Down Days

Craig Hallam

Inspired
Quill

Published by Inspired Quill: November 2019

First Edition

TW: Please note that the central theme of this book is living with depression and anxiety. There are also mentions of suicidal thoughts and medication.

Down Days © 2019 by Craig Hallam
Contact the author through his website: www.craighallam.wordpress.com

Chief Editor: Sara-Jayne Slack
Cover Design: Venetia Jackson
Typeset in Palatino

Paperback ISBN: 978-1-913117-00-9
eBook ISBN: 978-1-913117-01-6
Print Edition

Printed in the United Kingdom
1 2 3 4 5 6 7 8 9 10

Inspired Quill Publishing, UK
Business Reg. No. 7592847
www.inspired-quill.com

To everyone who read Down Days when it was a misspelled eBook on a deeply buried blog.

To those who shared, and visited, and supported.

To those who didn't give up so that I didn't either.

This book exists because of you.

You've done good.

Table of Contents

Introduction

THIS BOOK IS an exercise in stark honesty, and so here's a list of things that you *won't* find between these pages:

- You won't find any advice of the practical sort.
- I don't think the purpose of what you're about to read is meant to be uplifting.
- I'm certainly not going to concern myself with technical terms.
- This isn't intended as a self-help book (but I hope it will help, anyway).

Now we've talked about what this book isn't, let's talk about what it is.

What you *will* find is honesty. This is me, as I am; someone who is a fully-functioning adult with aspirations and loved ones. I also have what I call "Down Days". These are days when the world seems to peel away, leaving me a shivering, naked, fruity centre. I won't be blinding you with science, but I *will* be telling you how it actually feels to have depression. At least, I'll try. Because, as I'm sure you can imagine, it's a hard thing to describe.

What I'm about to share with you is extremely personal and the reason I'm writing it down is that it's easier. Behind this keyboard, it's easier. I'm quite happy hiding back here *thankyouverymuch*.

This book will be uneven. There will be days that I sit here, switched on and fiery with words spilling out of me. There will be Down Days. I'm going to try my damnedest to still write on those days. Because maybe, just maybe, you'll see something there that I can't describe. That's my hope.

For that reason, I won't be changing anything when I edit later. If I add something, it will be in square brackets [like this] so that you can see what I've done. No secrets.

There will be swear words. Swear words are expressive, beautiful things and I intend to use them.

I envisage that, if anyone reads this book at all, there might be two kinds of readers. One of them will be a lot like me. They will be dealing with some of the issues that I deal with, albeit their reasons and experiences will vary wildly. They will be looking for something – perhaps proof that they aren't alone.

The other kind will be The Interested. The people who are striving to know more. Perhaps they have loved ones like us, or work with them, or they're just curious.

Whichever you are, person dangling over this page, I'm sorry if the words fail me. I'll type words now that, at times, have the ability to make me cry if I say them out loud: I'm trying. Partly for you and partly for me.

For Those Like Me, I'm hoping I can find some words that you can use yourself. I know how hard it is to start a conversation, or even begin to describe to those who don't understand how you're feeling. If just one sentence of this book is useful to you, I'll consider this endeavour worthwhile. Hell, just hand that special person a copy of the book and let them read it for themselves. Some things are best said silently.

For The Interested, I hope you might gain a little insight into how it feels for someone like us. You've had these feelings yourself. Everyone has. But there's something extra about people with depression, isn't there? Something that makes it all come crashing down around them in a way you can't really understand. I have no idea what that *thing* is. But, if I describe it to you just right, maybe you'll figure it out and write your own book. Please do, because I'd really want to read it.

Here goes.

PART 1:

In which some heavy shit goes down

Buckets of anguish and teardrops on Kleenex.
Curled in a ball, try to fight off the bleakness.
Your mind has turned in the most horrid ways.
That's how it feels to have a Down Day.

—Lyrics from The Sound of Misery,
(my upcoming depression musical)

What makes me tick?

WHAT MAKES A depressive? There are plenty of theories. My favourite is that I'm just wrapped up this way. I swore I wouldn't go into too much personal detail when I started writing this book. I'm a pretty private person and so dirty laundry will not be aired. Plus, we're all so very different that my life story will be irrelevant to you. What triggers me might not trigger someone else. And what seems perfectly normal to you will drive me up the damned wall. But there are certain things that I think are a factor in my Down Days that might be relevant.

First, I have low self-esteem. This comes primarily from a parent berating me for being over-weight as a child. Continuously. For years. The same parent was constantly disappointed in me for not expressing my gender in the straightforward blue/pink, football/dollies kind of way. I'm a reader, a thinker, a writer. I'm your one-stop imagination station. Going outside to kick an inflatable seemed like a waste of time to me when there was knowledge to be had between the covers of a book. This, of course, is only how I remember it. I'm sure that parent would disagree, but the shape of the memories is what is important, and memory is tricksy.

The other thing which sucked as a kid, was that I was bright. *Not* academic (I wasn't great in school) but bright. There are reports that I was always talking to the adults rather than playing with the kids at parties. As I look back, I remember observing other kids more than interacting with them. I never really understood them, and in turn they didn't get me. I had mastered sarcasm by the time I was six. This isn't bragging; there's nothing special going on here. If you want to even it out, I couldn't tell the time until well after every other child, and I still squint at clocks a bit funny to this day. It's just how I'm built. And it explains why I spent a lot of time outside of my expected social circles.

You see the problem there, right?

I also learnt to evade bullies at an early age by talking my way out of tense situations. That led to the development of a self-deprecating sense of humour.

Bully: Oy shithead, your trackies are missing a stripe!

Translation into English: Hello person I see as beneath me. Are you aware that Adidas tracksuit bottoms, a pair of which I am currently sporting, have three stripes and, therefore, your tracksuit bottoms with only two are of a far less expensive variety and therefore I have further proof that you're a pile of manure?

Me: That's because I'm poor and useless and fat and

ugly and possibly whatever sexual orientation you find offensive.

There's no work for the bully to do if I do it for them, you see. The problem with that kind of thinking is that after a while you start to believe it yourself. I express my low self-esteem through humour, so people think I'm only joking. It still does the job of putting me out of the "threat to your masculinity" category, hence further away from the "stab him to make yourself feel better" repercussions, but also expresses how I feel about myself in a way which tricks people into feeling less weird about it.

But back to that whole "believing it yourself" thing. The brain likes repetition. The brain believes anything you tell it as long as you tell it that thing enough times. One way or another, my brain has been told that I'm overweight and useless, over and over, for years. So, you can hardly blame me when things start to go wrong and I naturally assume it's my fault. Or, when an attractive member of my preferred gender presents themselves and my pre-set mentality is to not bother.

Now low self-esteem is a big bag of dicks all on its own. But couple it with being brought up to always be independent (which leads to an insane amount of pridefullness (pretty sure I made that word up (Ooooh, brackets within brackets (bracket-ception!))) and a genuine belief that it would be so very easy to make the world a better place if people were just *nicer* to each other, you have:

A person who cares about the world too much, is physically angered by ignorance and arrogance, and who, when they get Down Days, won't tell anyone because they refuse to be a burden to others.

That's me in a nutshell. And it's a very shitty nutshell.

The Big Event

[This whole next chapter was added when I realised that I'd missed a lot of my Big Event story out and, despite not wanting to drain you with details, it was probably important to explain a little bit. I never planned to mention explicitly being a Nurse and you'll see why in a moment. Suffice to say that I have left that career now, and I won't ever go back. But it has torn a hole in my life, my personality, and my identity that still hurts. So, this chapter might be a bit sombre, as it still scares me to think about. Apologies in advance.]

T HIS SECTION IS the hardest to write. It sums up a time in my life that I find deeply embarrassing, and still makes me feel distraught to consider. Although I'm sure that I'm wrong, the nervous breakdown that I experienced a few years ago feels like a single point in my life despite there being symptoms of depression both before and after it. That sounds crazy, I know, but I pin the Big Event down to a single moment.

I was never going to talk about this, because, quite frankly, I'm a coward and I look back on my career as a Nurse not with pride at the good work that I did, but as a huge failure. I failed. Depression broke everything I had worked to achieve in my career. I've been told otherwise by many people, and I would do the same if the shoe was on the other foot.

Sometimes you just can't shake a feeling, and looking back at the last few years of my nursing career will always give me a sense of shame. The people, the work, everything. It wore me down.

I *let* it wear me down.

Anyway, we were talking about The Big Event itself. I sometimes call it The Crash, depending on how dramatic I'm feeling.

I sat outside my place of work, in my car, my uniform on and the engine running. I had minutes before my shift started. I couldn't move. I stared at my steering wheel, then at the door to the building only a few feet away, then at my hands and the lint on my trousers which it seemed really important that I get rid of before I left the car, then I turned on the windscreen wipers, because it seemed like the right thing to do despite the lack of rain. Then I reattached my seatbelt and drove away.

That's exactly how it happened. No specific thoughts in my head at all. Just a feeling of dread, and the realisation that I wouldn't be going through that door today. So, I drove home, and I dropped to my knees in the living room, and I literally (not figuratively, I know the difference) curled into a ball and stayed there all day. Nothing could have moved me. Not hunger, not needing to pee. Only when I heard my partner's car door slam outside did I move, the fear that she'd find me like that finally enough to get me up and moving.

That was the first day. There were so many more.

I know that sounds like so easy a story. All I did was shut off, right? Well, yes and no. You see, there were moments before that, now that I think back, which led to it. Moments of frustration at the place I was working, moments where things slipped my mind and my concentration was off. I would come home after a shift, not physically exhausted, but mentally. The whole day would play over and over in my head, every little thing said or done becoming a moment to obsess over. I would come home and cry, for no good reason, just a tear or two over my cup of tea or hidden from my partner in the kitchen. But that was no big deal, right? I knew I was unhappy and so that was normal. Hell, maybe that stoic nature of mine was starting to relax a little in my advancing years. Showing emotion is healthy, isn't it? So why worry?

I told myself a million such platitudes at the time but, I now know, in perfect 20/20 hindsight, that these were all the warning shots of a nervous breakdown.

I don't remember calling in sick to work, but I must have. I don't really remember the reason I gave them, or my partner for that matter. There was a month, a whole month of my life that's just snapshots of myself, like a cheesy movie montage, getting out of bed in the morning just to hug my knees on the sofa all day and then return to bed at night. Everything was gone, shut off. I had no higher functioning thoughts at all. Making any decision more complicated than when to pee was out of the question.

The Big Event turned out to be more of a void; a black hole that sucked in all the light around me so there's only darkness when I look back at it now. Maybe I should call it The Big Nothing instead.

Don't ask me why I didn't reach out for help. I don't know. Asking that question of someone who has no idea what their own mind was doing at the time is not only fruitless but heartless. I know this because I've been asked the same thing a hundred times, often by the same people over and over [managers, usually]. Some of whom I now, thankfully, never have to see again. These people demand explanations because they don't have any insight into mental health issues. They don't understand why simply repeating a question with increasing levels of pity in their voice doesn't yield some nicely bundled answer. A quote generally said to be from Einstein, but it isn't certain, goes like this:

"[Insanity is] doing the same thing over and over again and expecting different results."

What I do know is that, if the thought had occurred to me to ask for help, I wouldn't have been sure what to say anyway. I had no idea what was wrong with me. I was completely unprepared and my brain was cotton wool. It took a whole month of wraith-like wandering around my house to come to any conscious realisation that I was even ill. The whole thing was automatic, like a fever to fight off infection. My mind had shut down, leaving only my body's autopilot to move it around. I basically took anything my partner said as gospel and did whatever anyone told me to do.

At some point, I must have decided I should go to the doctor. I had this knot of an idea in my brain; I needed help and I needed it badly. A single moment of realisation, perhaps, that I was broken. I didn't know what was going on, but I knew that I couldn't get through it alone. I was also agonisingly afraid of admitting what I thought was the cause, that I was depressed and hadn't realised until it was too late.

It was maybe another month after the doctor's appointment before I could string sentences together again and actually consider, consciously, what I was saying. This sounds like it should be quite cool, like KITT taking over the driving for Michael Knight. But it isn't. It's scary as hell. My mind couldn't handle whatever was going on, and so it simply switched off, went into hibernation, hid until it was all over and the emotional swelling in my brain subsided. I could have said anything to anyone for those couple of months and had no idea afterward.

Do you know the *really* scary part? Almost no-one noticed there was anything wrong with me at all.

"Why don't we just sit here for a while, see what happens?"
—MacReady, *The Thing*

A decision without any options

L OOKING BACK, I know that my depression caused me to make mistakes, even before The Big Event taught me a crushing lesson about myself.

At one point, and I have no idea when it started, my depression began affecting my ability to think. Concentration became difficult, which led to memory lapses. As a result, I made mistakes. For someone like me who pretty much defines themselves based on their usefulness, it was a huge blow. And this was only the onset. Depression was just getting started. Soon after I couldn't go to work at all when The Big Event finally hit. I'd never felt anything like it before. The sky fell down around me.

Je suis Chicken Little.

In my usual style, I had tried to bottle this whole thing up, to hide it (my pride being high on my list of failings). And so, I held it in until it was too late. After the Big Event, when I finally took my Bambi steps back into the world, I was different. I had changed and not in a good way.

No human being can go through an experience like that and come out the other side shiny and new. I was no sleek Jaguar out of the showroom, I was a busted up 1989 Ford Festiva with mismatched doors and gaffer tape holding on the bumper. When I went back to work, I was still a nurse, only now I was even less equipped to deal with the stress of the job.

But what was I supposed to do? Leave? And pay my mortgage how, exactly?

As far as I could see it, I either stayed and hoped that I would get better despite the crushing stress and expectations that came with my work, or I walked away into the sunset. Either you function or you don't. You work or you're institutionalised. You have a job with a wage slip or you go homeless. This is not exaggeration. Where's the financial support for Those Like Me who can no longer function in their old lives after their brain does the Mental Mamba? If only short-term while you try to heal from a nervous breakdown or find other, less stressful work, there should be something, right? But it doesn't exist if you have no continence issues, need no help with preparing food, dressing, reading, or making financial decisions.

And so, I did the only thing I felt I could do. I stayed. I tried to soldier on. And, as a result, I watched my mental health take a dive into the bedpan.

"The mind commands the body and it obeys. The mind orders itself and meets resistance."

—St. Augustine of Hippo (Hehehe hippos are awesome)

The After Effects

I WENT BACK to work with the worst emotional hangover you can imagine. My mind remained unfocussed and became easily exhausted. For me, passing through such a crushing psychological event didn't leave me feeling cured or better. I wasn't interested in the fact that I had survived. Far from it. I could no longer trust myself. I'd had thoughts. Dark fucking thoughts. I had been rendered physically useless by a condition which had no right to affect me that way. It was in my head, so why was my body so weak? And, it pains me to say, those mistakes I'd made while affected by the condition were still mistakes made [for the record, no harm ever came to anyone under my care. Only clerical and organisational things slipped my mind]. Being me is annoying, because I refuse to duck responsibility for things that I've done wrong, even if, I figured out much later, I couldn't have done anything to stop it. The human mind is an incredible thing, we're told, but it's also fallible. I won't be shoving many quotes on you, but there's a neuroscientist called Dean Burnett who wrote an interesting and funny book about how the brain is fundamentally stupid as hell. I'll drop a reference at the end if you fancy reading it. What Burnett is getting at in his book is that, yes, the human mind is an incredible feat of evolutionary engineering. It also sucks (my words, not his). Everything we do is defined by the brain and Burnett describes that as:

"...a tangled mess of habits, traits, outdated processes and inefficient systems."

Yep. That sounds about right, actually. If you're sitting there, reading this, and you don't recognise something of yourself in that quote, then answer me one question:

What's it like observing humans from outside the species?

When you see the brain as a mass of misplaced wiring crammed into a broken old Atari casing, then you start to not only have a more realistic view of yourself, but you also begin to understand how the after-effects of depression might come about.

I had never had an anxiety attack in my life. I'm claustrophobic, and can get a little crazy when trapped, but never a full holy-crap-I'm-dying-for-no-good-reason anxiety attack. Since the Big Event, I now get the gremlins at odd intervals, sometimes with no justifiable cause at all. Where the hell did that come from? And my memory is still rubbish. I do more of the "what did I come in here for" and "putting your cup of tea in the fridge and taking the milk into the living room" kind of things than I ever did.

You're getting old, you might say.

I'm only thirty-two [at the time of writing this]! The cheek! Sheesh.

I'm more easily distracted, too. At one point, I would have sat here for hours on end, typing away without a care. Now, the slightest interruption knocks my concentration completely. This has nothing to do with mood and, I have no idea if this is right or not, but it just seems like the way my mind works has fundamentally changed.

Here's a thing for The Interested, I think. After the initial depression, symptoms remain that have *nothing* to do with mood. I don't lose concentration only when I'm having a Down Day. I also have the ability to be happy as a lark (which apparently are quite happy birds, who knew?)

Mood as you understand it has very little to do with my Down Days. These are not the 'normal' range of emotions we're talking about. These are debilitating psychological events. We just don't have a decent term other than 'mood' or 'feelings' to describe it and so it gets clubbed together into the same flim-flam kind of category. Just like the term 'psycho' has come to mean anyone violently bonkers when, in fact, there are perfectly functional and non-murdering psychopaths wandering around all over the place.

And, of course, there are the Down Days, which are separate and yet linked to all these other things (which we'll go into detail about a little later). They come as frequently as they please, without warning or reason. They have the ability to make me lie on the floor, exhausted by breathing, unable to think or move. It sometimes seems like the Big Event has weakened the gate in my mind as it burst out and now the damn thing is hanging off its hinges, letting any old rubbish saunter through when it feels like it.

My point is that depression isn't just sadness. It's the pied piper with a parade of nightmares marching behind.

PART 2:

In which I lighten up a bit

How do I even begin
to explain?

I THINK ABOUT poets quite often.

Don't worry, I'm not going to lecture you on the intricacies of poetry. But the poets themselves, I think about. They know how to do it, don't they? To get their emotions across in a way, using just the right words, so that you sit there, sometimes not even knowing what you're reading about, but you *get it*. You know exactly how that daffodil made them feel, or the loss of that loved one. One of my favourites to read is Plath (for obvious reasons). She knew how to get across the dual nature of a depressive's mind. I'm not saying Plath is a role model. She had more than her share of shit and took the road that she felt needed to be taken (we'll talk about suicide later). But she also knew how to take what we depressives have been taught to hide, and gave it a tangible form.

When I read *Tulips* for the first time, I thought *Yes! That's it!* and I could have stood up on the bus, stabbing at the page with my finger and screamed at my fellow travellers. I didn't, obviously. But I bloody well felt like it.

When you get that connection, when you look up at that person as you pour your soul out through your eye sockets, and you realise they're nodding at you, that feeling can turn your world around. That's how I felt when I read *Tulips*. Like Plath was nodding at me with understanding in her eyes.

It took me a long time to talk about my depression. There were a lot of reasons for that. I felt unprepared, unskilled for the task of expressing the kind of raw emotion that some people have never felt. Movies show you how to deal with love on a cosmic scale. You run to the airport and scream a cheesy one-liner over a barrier and get dragged away by security only to have your intended come back at the last minute and say that they didn't get on the plane. Or you can just buy flowers or something, I guess. Anyway, movies show us how to be happy, how to be brave and overcome, how to fight fucking dragons. They sure as shit don't tell us how to express depression.

The sad thing is, a lot of folks out there learn everything they know through watching TV. But, the Glowing Window of Joy is failing us.

Watch any tabloid talk show and you will see inarticulate people screaming at each other over family feuds, expressing the hell out of their emotions on live television. Listen to them. How do they talk? They talk in clichés.

"I'd do anything for my babies."

"I just want you to be a father to my babies."

"I swear on my babies' lives!"

(There's an awful lot of talk about babies, as it turns out.)

They say things that they've heard on soap operas and in films, repeating them word for word and not even realising it, because that's how they've learnt to communicate; mostly by shouting. We learn by watching, as we have since we were children. And those people watch a shit-ton of television just like the show they're appearing on (It's the ciiiircle of liiiiife).

But what do we depressives have? What example of human anguish can I watch to learn the skills I *need* to get it across to my loved ones that I'm depressed?

My point is, how are we supposed to convey the unconveyable? (I made that word up as well).

I said very little, when the time came.

I sat in the doctor's office, on a chair that didn't even hold my full weight. Not really. There's all thirteen stone [and then some] of my actual weight, and that chair took it like a champ. But I could feel the *other* weight, too, the one that crushed my shoulders down toward my knees, the one that twisted my back and shoved my eyes down at the ground all at once. That chair couldn't possibly hold every ounce of that weight as well. Luckily, that extra weight exists in an alternate dimension that only I have the ability to perceive. A useless superpower if there ever was one.

Anyway, I sat there feeling the weight of a universe unseen pressing down on me and the Doctor asked me if he could help. That's how he put it.

"Can I help?"

All I could think was: "How do I tell him? What do I say?"

Saying that I felt depressed just didn't come to my mind. At all. And even if it had, I don't think I'd have said it. The phrase seems so hollow, overused. The terms 'depressed' and 'stressed' are thrown around so often now, it almost seems that we're not allowed to use them any more for the fear of people just rolling their eyes. But screaming, "I'm angry and tired and hungry and grieving for something I haven't lost. I can feel my life leaking out of me, my survival instinct has gone and left me alone with every mistake I've ever made like a mudslide in my head," didn't seem right either, or fair to the poor guy.

And that's when I raised my eyes. I don't think I'd even looked at him until that point. Not when I walked in or when I sat down, not even when he said hello. I vaguely remembered him asking me how I was, now I think back, and I swear I just said I was ok on reflex. But then came the moment when he asked if he could help and I finally looked up at him and said:

"I don't know."

The tears didn't just fall. My whole body gave one huge spasm and I bloody erupted. That poor doctor. That poor *kid*. He couldn't have been out of training for more than a week, the way he looked, and a grown adult had just exploded in the seat before him. But you know what? That kid gave me a look that I never knew I needed.

He just nodded. And he didn't say a damn thing.

Over the years, people have told me any number of variations on the following:

- Just calm down
- It'll be ok
- Don't worry
- You have so much good stuff going on

None of those things have ever helped. In fact, (here's a conundrum for you) I find that encouragement breaks me faster than a bastard ever will. How messed up is that? Depression isn't a pantomime. There will be no audience participation.

Now, where did that depression monster go?
He's behind you!

I actually try to tell people to please not join in when I'm on a Down Day. Don't list all the beautiful baskets-of-kittens-farting-rainbows things that I should be focussing on. When something goes badly, please don't get angry on my behalf, either. Please don't tell me that I'm not letting you down when I finally do get it out in words. Please, just please, don't tell me you love me in that moment. That just makes the tears come even harder.

But that doctor's silence and encouraging nod was exactly what I needed. I swear, I've had friends just put a hand on my shoulder and say nothing at all while I weep, and I've felt more comforted than after any conversation.

Sometimes words just fail.

The world doesn't work that way, of course. We communicate through words. Poets just write theirs down, that's all. They have skills that the rest of us don't. They also have the time to draft that perfect expression. Try doing the same off-the-cuff with a head full of cotton wool made of pure anguish, with your face stinging like wasps have been on the attack, and you might find yourself less coherent.

How do you get that out? I think I started to say: "I just feel—" and then nothing would come.

In the years that followed, I've gotten better. In times when I've not seen a Down Day for a while, and I have the time to think about what makes me tick, I have come up with a few choice phrases that I use to get it across. At first I used to simply say: "You wouldn't understand. It's ok." Until I realised that I was being as bad as those people who just talked at you like their heartfelt opinion was going to somehow soothe your soul. How annoyingly arrogant of them, and how arrogant of me to presume that someone wouldn't understand. I wasn't doing myself or anyone else any favours. And so, I stopped saying that. I tried to describe, in a meandering kind of way, how I knew very well that things might not be as bad as I felt them to be, but that's how I felt regardless.

Now, I use two approaches when I try to tell someone what it's like to have depression.

First, I tell people that it's like watching a movie. Whatever your favourite kind might be. Mine's horror so we'll go with that for now, but it works for every genre.

I watch horror because it's fun to be scared. Lots of people feel the same way. When I watch Freddy stalking some disposable teen, or the latest spooky ghost film, what do I do? I wait for the scares. I know they're coming, and of course I know that none of it is real, and yet my pulse races and I still jump out of my seat like an idiot.

That's a lot like depression.

I already know everything you can possibly tell me about my life. I really do. List all the things I'm lucky to have over the course of several days, if you like, but the emotional response is still there. For Those Like Me, it's as automatic as crying at the end of *Sleepless in Seattle* (not that I do that…obviously). I know that the horror movie isn't real, but I will still jump at the scary parts.

My second favourite explanation is the Two-Mes, which is how I describe the feeling of lack of control.

It's a lot like there are two of me. One of me is the practical one who moves around and does things, the other is stood just behind my right shoulder and giving guidance. One is the body, one is the mind, if that helps. Now, a lot of the time, they are both in tandem about everything I do, whether I'm washing the pots or writing this book. But, on my Down Days, they forget how to get along. The me in front is sat with their knees up under their chin, eyes scrunched closed, and in their head is a flurry of negativity. Every mistake ever made, every argument where I was wrong, the time I tripped and embarrassed myself in class when I was nine years old. But also, the small things, the people who've been mean in front of me and it's riled me up, that one time an ignorant old lady shoved past me in the queue, that little snarky comment that the bully at work made that I just can't shake. All those things are crashing around Me Number One and they're so loud that no matter how much Me Number Two shouts, the other can't hear. I can see what I'm doing but I can't stop myself.

When I first went to the doctor, I had neither explanation in my arsenal. He got it, anyway. As I sat there and cried, I could have washed my hands with the tears that fell on them. But he talked straight. There were options: help I could have, people to talk to, people to listen. There were treatments that might help me get over the worst of it. All of this washed over me until he asked the worst question of all:

"Have you had any suicidal thoughts?"

Oh shit.

"You wake up one morning, afraid that you're going to live."
—Prozac Nation *(Not* an uplifting movie)

The fateful decision

HAVE YOU EVER thought about ending it all? Taking your own life? Harming yourself? Horrible euphemisms, the lot of them. But they're necessary, I suppose.

For those of a more squeamish nature who prefer those euphemisms, I'm sorry for dropping the idea of (ready for this one?) auto-euthanasia (*bleurgh*) in without warning you. But it turns out that this is going to be a stream of consciousness kind of thing and, well, it came up.

Personally, I still prefer the term 'committing suicide'. Not only does it say what it means, but the idea of committing to something, even suicide, just seems like a better image to me than anything medical or metaphorical. It feels less flaky. Because people do think of me and Those Like Me as special little snowflakes who melt on the breeze. We ain't. Walking around and being a functional adult when you can feel the gravitational pull of the planet dragging down your every footfall is damned hard work. For those who progress toward thoughts of suicide, it's a hard decision to make. It's a commitment that there's no divorce from a few months or years down the line. It isn't something that someone does on a whim, no matter whether you can understand it or not.

I have thought about suicide. I won't bore you with the details, but it has crossed my mind an awful lot. Hell, as I write this, on a day that will mean nothing by the time this book is finished, I thought about it. I've gone over every option, thought it out, researched where to buy the damn supplies. But I never have.

So, as I sat in the Doctor's office, he slid a form toward me. He told me to be as honest as possible and to take my time. It was the hardest quiz I've ever taken and I already knew the answers.

As it turns out, there are numbers attributed to these things. After a little maths, he asked me that fateful question. I knew why he was asking. He had to gauge if more help was required to make sure I 'didn't do anything silly' (that one is particularly galling). I had, so I nodded. He asked what the likelihood of me going ahead with it was (which seems like an arbitrary thing to do, now I think about it). I told him, and I quote:

"I'm too much of a chicken shit."

Because that's how it felt; like committing suicide would be a fine solution, if only I could pluck up the courage. Now, I'm going to say something here that I don't want you to misunderstand. Some things need to be said and never are, so I'm going to do it and hope it doesn't backfire.

Suicide, for some, is the only option. It is not some casual impulse, or an act of selfishness. Suicide, for those who really mean it, who really need it, comes from a belief that the world would be better without that person in it. It is the only way to put an end to an incomparable amount of pain. Overriding the human urge to survive takes bravery and forethought, not cowardice.

Now, saying that, *I am not suggesting that suicide is the only solution.* I'm not even saying that it's a good idea.

I am only suggesting that no one should have the audacity to judge someone else's state of mind.

Also, those who harm others in their search for suicide are an anomaly, and everyone with any sense knows that that is wrong.

Anyway, the Doc said that I could have some medication if I liked and that he'd sign me up for a counsellor if that was what I wanted. I just nodded to everything at that point. With an appointment in one hand and a box of pills in the other, I went home.

"No, I'm fine. Just wish I were dead, that's all."
—*A Gentleman's Agreement* (a very old film)

The Council of One

THAT TITLE SEEMS a little ominous, now I read it, but it's also a bit Game of Thronesy so I'll leave it.

You know what? Before I even took those pills, I felt better. Those tears seemed to have chased away the fog in my head. I'd fought those damned tears for ages. I felt a little silly. I debated whether I needed the tablets at all, or whether I should just cry more regularly. Such is depression. Me Number Two stepped up behind me and, thankfully, we decided together that I was going to take them anyway, at least until the appointment in my other hand.

To save some time here, the counsellor and I didn't get on. I had three sessions with her before I realised that she couldn't tell me anything I hadn't already read in a book. This is by no means a reason for you to not have counselling. As was proven to me a couple of years later when I tried counselling again, after another particularly bad Down Day which turned into a series of months. All counsellors are not created equal. But that first counsellor was a whale-song and meditation type. She clearly had no idea that, for someone like me, spending *more* time in my own head would be devastating. She also didn't care in the slightest about my individual situation. As far as she was concerned, those whale song CDs worked for every one of her patients. EVERY ONE. Without fail. And all I needed to do was give myself a good shake and it would all be okay. I started to see that the Mrs Trunchbull School of Counselling had a single member, and I was stuck in a room with her.

The second counsellor was bloody brilliant. She was a listener, as all good counsellors are. Not so full of suggestions and notions, and more inclined to let me come to my own conclusions. That was the kind of counselling I needed. After watching enough episodes of *Frasier*, some of the things that a psychologist or counsellor will say, have become cliché. We even laughed about it a little, actually, the first time she asked me: "How does that make you feel?" But after the laughter, the question remained. How *does* it make me feel?

How does it make you *feeeeeeeel*?

Jeez. That's the big question we all get asked. And how you'd say the answer to your loved ones or doctor, or your pet iguana if that works for you, won't be the same thing that I would say. I'm certain, after coming across a host of others with depression since mine took hold, that not a single one of my friends, relatives, co-workers or members of the public ever feels it exactly the same.

I would never cut myself, for instance. For some, it's the

go-to way for releasing tension. For me, it's a horizontal weeping session that does the trick. Or I pace. On occasion, I write bad poetry (if you're unlucky I'll put some at the back of this book so you can see exactly how bad). I have been known, when alone in bed, unable to move at midday, to scream and stamp my feet against the mattress with the sheer frustration of it all. Such a childish, tantrum-like thing to do, I know. And I hate admitting it. But I swore I'd be honest, and so I am.

Bearing in mind that the medication was probably helping me along when I was sat in front of that counsellor, I managed to get through it without crying. Plus, I'd had a poet's amount of time to think on what I might say. It went something like:

"Like I'm worthless. Like my life is one long session of plaiting fog. Like I'm just staving off hunger and death, living by force of habit. I'm so very aware of my own mortality and how small and insignificant I am. I know that, in less than fifty years after my death, no one would have cause to remember my name. And, for some stupid reason, that all matters to me."

For some stupid reason. I know that is wrong, now, but it felt right to say it at the time.

Here's the thing about counselling: it's something that we all do every day, for our loved ones and friends, the old guy on the bus who insists on sharing his life story unasked for, and most of us suck at it. If I can pass on one thing for you to hang on to, it's this:

You can't always help. Sometimes you just have to wait. Advice isn't your greatest gift, *patience* is.

There's also a line not to be crossed here. Those Like Me are allowed to say that what they're feeling is stupid. Everyone else isn't. Think of it as a psychological 'N' word. This isn't because we're precious. It's because later, when the manure hits the windmill, we won't remember that we said it about ourselves. But we will remember that *you* said it. Because that's how the depression monster works. He saves things like that in his Tupperware lunchbox for his next visit, and he brings each one out and shares them in gory detail with us before snaffling them up.

Magic Pills

S O, I DID the doctor/counselling/medication thing. That all started a long time ago. I've since come off the medication. Here's one of the few moments of practical advice I'll give you. I want you to read the next sentence, then read it again, then say it out loud:

Never. EVER. Stop taking your medication without your doctor's advice.

I did this the *first* time I tried to stop taking them. I learnt my lesson. Do you know how anti-depressive medication works? It alters your brain chemistry. That's why it's brilliant. It literally changes how you feel from the inside. The downside of this is that coming off of the meds needs to be slow. Careful. Cautious. Doctors may not always understand your exact predicament, but they know pharmacology better than you do (unless you're a pharmacologist, of course, but even then, your mind isn't exactly clear on Down Days).

The effect of me coming off my meds without a doctor's help was that I became ill. Very, very ill. I will not exaggerate when I say that it remains in the top 5 scariest moments of my entire life, and I once drove a high-speed motorbike into a barbed wire fence so…you get the idea.

I literally could not move. I remember the cold, creeping sensation of being lowered into an ice bucket. Every breath was like being water boarded; drowning without the blessed relief of death. *That* is how it felt to be an idiot and stop taking my medication.

Do not do it.

It took almost a month of being back on the medication before I could function again, and not just exist as a husk that people kept feeding and watering. A houseplant had more functional skills than me. And then it was two years before I dared to try again. *With the doctor's help.*

So why come off the meds at all?

Well, my reasons were two-fold. One, as I mentioned earlier, I'm a prideful sod. I wanted to know that I *could* get along and function just fine without pharmacological assistance. But, when I'm honest, it was the second thing that did it for me.

The one thing that frustrated me more than anything while taking the medication was that my productivity took a nose-dive. I like to write. I find it cathartic. I spend more time in my fantasy worlds than the real one because the real one sucks. But on that medication, the words wouldn't come. So ironically, my coping mechanism vanished. The one kind of counselling that truly, consistently worked for me, the medication took away. That seemed counter-productive. I grew more frustrated with myself, the book I was working on stopped dead, and that, for me, was hell of Pin-Head proportions.

So, I stopped taking them (under medical supervision, of course). Medication works for a lot of people out there. To help them sleep, to help them get up, to even out their mood and help them cope on a day to day basis. For a lot of reasons, medication can be a real life-saver. It just wasn't for me long-term. I don't want any of Those Like Me to think I'm making a case against the meds. I'm not. When I was at my very worst and needed something to even me out so that I could get through, the medication helped me to do that. I can't be certain, but I think that if I hadn't taken them, I would have gone irredeemably off the deep end. Thoughts of suicide, thoughts of just running away from my job, my life, my partner and my responsibilities. I had them all. But the meds meant that Me Number Two remained in earshot. I could make it through.

However, I'm off them now. It's the only reason that I can sit down and write what you're reading with any clarity. And I'm not even convinced I'm managing that yet.

[I never thought this book would be sent to a publisher, so I used emoticons if I bloody well wanted to].

"—live in peace, or pursue your present course and face obliteration. We shall be waiting for your answer; the decision rests with you."

—Klaatu, *The Day The Earth Stood Still*

Learning to manage

I T TURNS OUT that even though I didn't know it, I had symptoms of depression long before The Big Event. It turns out I had a lot of reasons. No one becomes depressed and collapses to the ground in a weeping pile because they've run out of milk. That comes later (been there) and is a symptom, not a cause. We all have our causes.

A cause is different to a trigger. A cause is the root of your depression, a trigger is something that sends you spiralling again (look at me, getting all technical). Perhaps we had some psychological trauma as a kid, perhaps we never learnt to deal, perhaps we just care too damn much and take everything personally. It's the way we're wired.

I am no doctor. I have zero credentials to talk about depression in a formal manner. All I have are my experiences, which have led me to the firm belief that depression is not an illness that can be cured. It would be like trying to cure someone's enjoyment of salted caramel, or the fact that cotton wool makes you get that weird feeling in the back of your mouth. We don't get cured; we learn to manage it. This comparison may piss some people off, but it's like cancer in the way that we don't talk about 'being cured', instead, we 'go into remission'.

For all my bad luck and bad judgement, this is where I am now. This is who I am. I'm not going away anytime soon. And so, I learn to manage myself.

Becoming self-aware is my greatest task. No amount of working toward a career or a family or a best-selling work of fiction (I'm still holding out for that) will ever compare to my learning about myself. I don't want to get Buddhist on you, but some of the things they say make an awful lot of sense. I began to think about myself. Not in the usual way of "look at all the shit that's happening to you", but actually about *me*. I tried to be honest with myself. I wrote things down. I have a notebook called "Craig's Depression". I shit you not.

What I realised is that I'm a normal human being. We are so desperate to be defined by our positive traits that we're taught to bottle the rest up. That's unhealthy. I'm not saying my occasional urge to punch a rude person in the face should be encouraged. I mean that I shouldn't be beating myself up about the odd inappropriate thought.

My friends, Those Like Me and The Interested, we are human bloody beings. We can't be good all the time. I often see things too logically and make decisions based on my principles when it isn't really appropriate. These are my failings and I've developed enough self-awareness to know when I'm doing them. So, I try not to be a cold, practical robot as much as possible. But, when I fail, be damned if I'll beat myself up about it. I just try again. From the beginning.

Why is the beginning seen as such a terrible thing to start from? The beginning is the best part. Tell me the first bite of ice cream doesn't taste better than every one that comes after it. The first few months of a relationship are always filled with such fire and intensity. The beginning has potential. Every time I have a Down Day, I get a new beginning. I reset the sign in my head that reads: 'X days since last incident', and I get to start fresh.

With every Down Day, you've learnt something. Every new beginning is a new life, but you remember the previous one.

"If only I knew then what I know now," people say.

Well you can do that. You can learn to manage better and better with every passing Down Day. I've learnt a few things that help me. These may be of no use to you at all, but it's important that The Interested see that Those Like Me can never truly switch off, never let their guard down. We're constantly on guard so that we can use our management tactics at any given moment. That can be in the middle of a conversation with our boss, while out drinking with our friends, buying a loaf of bread, or while listening to the Beastie Boys.

First, I'm getting better and better at recognising when a Down Day is coming. This one is particularly important as forewarned is forearmed. Most of the time, there's no avoiding it, but at least with the iceberg in sight you can brace for impact.

Sometimes I *can* do something to take the edge off.

Know something is causing my dip? Then I stop what I'm doing, or do something else. Getting cabin fever? I get out. People getting on my wires? Then I leave. I make my excuses and find somewhere quiet to be. Because, although being polite in society is what we should all strive to be, that doesn't mean you have to put up with people's shit.

People's expectations are quicksand. They won't hold you up and, trying to escape them, you'll quickly find yourself drowning.

This has occasionally led to me being seen as anti-social. I will often say to my partner, "I'm not going there, they do my head in." This isn't me just being a dick (okay, maybe sometimes), it's more about the fact that, as a person, I lack an internal monologue at the best of times. However, when I'm around stupidity, arrogance or ignorance, the already tissue-paper thin wall around my ability to keep my mouth shut just dissolves. I can't help it. It's an after-effect of the bullying as a kid. Now I'm older, all the fucks I had to give have long since passed into the Grey Havens, and I can't stand by and watch people be like that. I can, on occasion, have a mouth on me. And if I say I don't want to be around someone, it's because I know they're an idiot and I refuse to put myself in that situation. Why should I? Because, after they've said their racist/bigoted/stupid thing, and I've shot them down (or bit my tongue), they go on with their lives unchanged, because they're arrogant and ignorant (I'm going to coin the phrase "agnorant" henceforth). Me, on the other hand, it affects for much longer. Because I'm a depressive, and things like that stick with me. I refuse to be weighed down by these people. [Rant over. Sorry.]

Next up is being honest. There will be someone you can talk to. Someone you live with perhaps, or your parents. If you feel a Down Day coming on, tell someone. Don't feel the need to explain something that you don't have the words for, but communicate *something*. I find a very simple: "I'm having a Down Day," works best for me. My partner gives me the knowing nod and leaves me alone, because I usually genuinely *do* want to be left alone. All you have to do is adapt it to suit your situation.

"I'm having a Down Day so…"

1. Can we talk?

2. I'm going to get some air.

3. I'm going to back-to-back some Firefly episodes until I feel better.

And then there's the hardest part. Bringing yourself back to centre.

I hate this bit. Especially if I've gotten really comfy in my pillow fort. But, once the worst is over, you have to peek at that manure pile of a world and, with a deep breath, head on out again.

Your Down Day is over. Reset the counter. You survived.

It's a cycle of management, I think. And everyone will manage each step in their own way. Some people will struggle to spot the Down Day approaching; others find it hard to be open and not embarrassed about what they're dealing with to the point that they can just say when they're dipping; some folks need a Batman-style grappling hook to get themselves back out of their safe place. But each time, you will learn – if you keep trying. You don't even have to succeed. But you *do* have to try. And if you're about to ask "why try?", then I think finding your answer to that should be the first self-awareness lesson that you teach yourself, because the answer can't come from someone else, believe me.

"I am terrified by this dark thing that sleeps in me."
—Sylvia Plath, *Elm*

Trusting Me

[A quick section, this one. More of a thought I was having while trying to think of a way to describe this sensation. For the record, this isn't at the tip of my brain all the time. It comes and goes. However, when it is here, it feels like it's been there all along. Now, go ahead and read. Sorry for interrupting, urm, myself.]

C AN YOU IMAGINE how it feels to not be able to trust yourself?

It's like you're living in a body that you're sharing with another entity who hates the hell out of you, and you never know what they're going to do with your hands. This sidesteps conscious thought and reasoning. This is completely beyond my control. I find myself, to this very day, squinting at myself every morning, looking for some sign of this other bastard hidden away in there. Is this the day he takes over? He shows me images all the damn time.

Right on the tip of my brain. Flashes of dark things that are too fast, too deep, to avoid. How long before he pushes just enough to make something happen?

I scare myself. I don't trust me. Because when it's here, I'm not.

Any day that isn't a Down Day is one of the other kind, where I'm waiting. I'll never trust myself again. Not properly. I've learnt the lesson that, for all I try, I can never be in full control of what happens in my head. And that is petrifying.

When your mind shows you images of every option for ending yourself how are you supposed to trust it? That version of you isn't a visitor. It lives inside like a heckler at a stand-up comedy show, just waiting for you to pause so that it can throw something debilitating at you.

That scares me. I am constantly afraid.

How do you manage that?

"Wise men speak because they have something to say;
fools because they have to say something."

—Plato

Apologies for philosophy

I'VE BEEN THINKING about the medication that I mentioned earlier. I think I might have missed out a huge piece of the puzzle, and so I'm going back to it. Sorry.

Medication makes you feel better. It keeps you even. For me, I felt it dulled my emotions but that's kind of the point of it. It changed the way I thought, as it was supposed to, but there were days while I was taking medication where I wondered if it was the meds that were making me feel better, or whether I was *actually* better. How do I know if what I'm feeling and thinking is me or the little yellow tablet that I take every morning? And, for someone who actually *thinks* about this stuff, does that make me *me* anymore. Or am I someone different now?

This is purely philosophical, I'm sure, but the thought is there. Possibly my "know thyself" self-discovery makes me think about things a little too hard when there is simply no need or benefit. The question of whether my depression affects my decisions still remains, though.

I'd say yes. Of course, it does. I am now a different person to who I was five years ago. Completely different. My whole life philosophy has changed. I've taken a sidestep around the statue of my life and I'm seeing it from a new angle. My partner has said to me, in the past: "But you said [insert previous opinion] before," and I have to break it to her that I've changed my mind. I don't think like that anymore. The Big Event changed me.

That has had a profound effect on my outlook as a person. I now live for the moment a lot more. I have never really worried about people's ideas of convention, but now I care even less. I will do what I want, when and how I want. A following example is something that really winds me up. Some people prefer to think that everyone's lives go in set stages. Birth, grow up, get a career that will take you to retirement, get engaged, get married, have a kid, die. That is hideously depressing to me. And I find people's audacity for asking you when you will hit the next imaginary milestone to be utterly disgusting. I have actually started to tell people who ask when I'm going to have kids: "I'm infertile, but thanks for bringing it up." That shuts them right up. You can have that one for free. You're welcome.

While others are leaping the hurdles of their lives, Those Like Me are crushed under our doubts.

How do I know if the decisions I make are really me, or some sliver of the depression talking? How can I make the decision to have a child if I can't trust myself to think clearly? What if I have a Down Day and I'm looking after a five-month-old? What if I can't move and the poor kid is crying? What if they're hungry and their father is a useless husk that day?

How am I supposed to be a role model? Kids learn by watching, as I said before. They watch their parents and learn how to be well-rounded adults. How am I supposed to raise a well-rounded adult when I'm not one myself some days? Kids don't pick and choose what they learn, and I can't hide my nature forever.

What if I pass on my personality traits to that child genetically? How selfish would it be for me to knowingly set them up for a life of misery just so that I can say I have procreated? More importantly, what if the poor little bugger looks like me as well? Unfathomable misery for that kid, that's what. Don't I have some kind of social responsibility? If not to the world at large, to weed out whatever genetic twist that causes my brain to function this way, but to that non-existent child as well. [For the record, this kind of thinking is totally unhelpful and is not representative of my life philosophy at all].

I know that everyone takes a hurdle to the chest from time to time. But for a mind like mine some inherent feeling of duty to something that doesn't even exist, something intangible and yet overpowering, can stall the mind and set it into a constant loop of indecision and doubt. I feel nauseous, right now, as I write this, like I've drank bad milk, and it's my future I'm thinking about. How are Those Like Me supposed to plan and move through the world when every step we take opens up another path of crushing doubt? I wish I could learn to just crawl under the hurdle and head toward the next.

Almost a diary entry

[Another short one, I'm afraid. There is something to consider here, The Interested, about how Those Like Me deal with day-to-day things like jobs].

DEPRESSION HAS AFFECTED my life choices. For example, as I write this, I'm in a dilemma. What you've read so far has been mostly about catching you up. Now, we're in the present [although by the time you read this, it will be the past again. WEEEEIIIRD].

I have just left the job that I mentioned before. It has taken me years of striving, of trying to make it work, before I finally bit the bullet and left. This is partially because I've tried to get jobs and failed (often with an associated Down Day attached) and partially because I'm scared. I have no job to go to after this. I sit here, waiting out my notice, aware that some void stands before me.

This is a major life choice. But have I taken leave of a

place because I am ready? Or is it because I'm in the middle of a massive slump? This Down Day has lasted almost two weeks, but I felt it coming before that. I felt the pressure getting to me, I felt my concentration starting to slip. What am I supposed to do? There's no way of going to a doctor and saying, "I can feel it coming on" and expecting them to do something about it. I do my little tasks, long-since learned in counselling sessions. I listen to my music and do my writing. Hell, I even go to the gym [this did not last long, however] and actually started to enjoy it [and then I stopped enjoying it]. And so, what can a doctor do? The big changes, the deep-down changes that really matter, are up to *me*.

Sometimes, just sometimes, nothing will stop that Down Day from rolling right over you. Every time I feel a Down Day on the horizon, should I go sick? How would that work? Seriously, if you know, please tell me, because I don't know an employer who would put up with that.

People do not understand how mental health issues work. If you don't have some physical representation of your condition, then you either aren't ill at all or people regard you as a hair-trigger magnum .45. In a world where we are increasingly treated as numbers, defined by what money we can make rather than our personality, as robots for the controlling rather than people with intuition and ingenuity, and seen as the title of our social, ethnic, sexual or whatever category rather than our name and personality, then how do Those Like Me get by on the day-to-day?

We need a change of perspective in the general populace.

We don't want some heavy-handed government initiative that creates more categories for us to be put into so that workplaces and society can know how to "deal with" us when we crop up. We don't need a "How To Handle A Depressive" flow chart. Society needs to be educated. As with feminism, gay rights, racism and any other 'ism you can think of, it's all about education. It's about representation of Those Like Me in the media. Tell me the last time that someone with depression was in a newspaper without them having killed someone, themselves, or had gone off the reservation completely in a pants-on-their-head loony outburst. Tell me the last time that the news discussed depression where mental health wasn't seen as a flashpoint or a statistic. We don't need another insider documentary that only a small group of people will care to watch. Where are the lovable depressives on Coronation Street where people will actually see them?

*"It is possible to commit no mistakes and still lose.
That is not a weakness; that is life."*

—Captain Jean-Luc Picard,
Star Trek: The Next Generation.
(Also paraphrased by Beyoncé, so it must be true).

Back to the doctor

I WENT TO my doctor today. I've been feeling particularly low for some time and, despite not knowing what they could possibly do, it felt like I should mention it to someone. So, I talked to him. He didn't get it (this is a different doctor to last time. As with counsellors, so with doctors regarding consistency). He asked me if I'd been employing the techniques I'd learnt in counselling. I said yes. I had. And then he gave me what I like to call the "pat on the head". The part where he tells me to come back in two weeks and see if I feel better. I just want to scream:

"I could be fucking dead by then!"

But I didn't. Because I'm tired today, and just walking from the car into the surgery was an effort of herculean proportions. Instead, he asked if I wanted to go on medication again to which I said no. And so, I am now being treated "non-pharmacologically" which apparently, in doctor terms, means a shrug followed by a noise reminiscent of Scooby Doo saying "I don't know":

Rirunno.

Because that's literally what he did when I asked him what it meant.

And so, I'm back home now, typing my heart out and not really knowing what I'm writing. I expect when I read this back it'll make no damned sense. It's an odd sensation, actually, talking to someone in your head and not knowing if they'll ever hear it. I'm speaking right now, on paper, and I have no idea whether you're reading it. What an odd thought.

Anyway, let me make this a little better.

While I was in the waiting room earlier, I had a silly moment. I have this thing where I'm constantly on the cusp of crying. I've had it for a few weeks. I've had it before, and it comes and goes pretty frequently. At one point in my life, there was only one thing that could make me cry; the scene in *Dumbo* when his mum cradles him in her trunk through the cell door. Over the last few weeks, though, it can be bloody anything. Adverts, movies, finding I'd used the last sponge for the washing up. But today was a particularly brilliant example. Sat in the waiting room with me was a young mum and her son. The kid must have been five or six, I think. I have no gauge on these things. Anyway, he wanted his mum to read him a book from the pile of discarded hand-me-downs on the shelf. It was a Disney book about Mickey and Goofy flying a kite.

His mum read it out, the kid loved it. I sat there, trying my damnedest not to listen. Until the part where Mickey and Goofy befriend a little boy who doesn't have a kite, and share it with him.

I lost my shit.

Thank God I came packing tissues because I turned toward that window so no one could see, and cried my eyes out like a boss.

That has been my day. Hope it made you chuckle. Thinking back, it gives me one. Sometimes you need to laugh at yourself to stay sane. That's what all the pixies in my head keep telling me.

Use somebody

I KNOW, THAT title is a Kings of Leon song. It just popped into my head as I started this section.

So, it's now a couple of weeks after the previous doctor's encounter. I know, I said I'd try to write regularly but other things have gotten in the way, as they sometimes do.

I'm feeling a little more even again. I can think in straight lines once more. I've even managed a few nights of relatively undisturbed sleep. I'm on to a winner, it seems. I got to thinking, as I read back through what I've put down so far, about the part where I just dropped in that I went to the doctors, the first time around. The one with the young, understanding doctor. How did I get to that point? I made it sound so easy! It wasn't.

How do you choose the person that you can talk to? I dropped lucky with that first doctor. But what if you aren't at that stage yet? What if all you have are the people around you? Choosing your confidant is damned hard.

At first, I found myself walking around, kind of huddled over like an abused Victorian street urchin just expecting to be beaten. I watched people out of the corner of my eye, I listened to how they talked and what they said to better gauge how they would react if I decided to drop a whole ton of emotional crap on them, completely without warning. I say this without meaning any disservice to the people in my life. The people I have around me are there for a reason. They're great. But no one is inherently designed to be able to tackle someone else's emotional problems. When I was doing my reconnaissance, I didn't find anyone who I thought would be good to talk to. Not really. Everyone was too eager to advise. I needed a listener. My partner, bless her, likes to look at a problem and fix it. Done. Nothing I was struggling with could be fixed like that. My mum is a supporter but only through talking at you. She always wants to say something to you to make you feel better. It's a lovely sentiment, but for me it just doesn't work.

There was another element, too. I didn't want to be a burden. Not to my partner, who had her own crap to deal with. Not to my mum. They were too close to everything. I needed someone unbiased, someone for whom, when I said that I was unhappy with my life, wouldn't take it as a personal insult. I needed a friend.

Looking back, I now realise that a mistake was made in finding who I talked to. I want to admit to you all that I made that mistake, and show you how. You see, as I mentioned before, when you're in a down period you don't always make good choices. You make them based on emotion, or the lack thereof. What you might think is logic is actually deeply flawed. This is a little to do with depression but entirely due to being human. Perhaps I can help you avoid it, though. Also, don't let my mistake scare you away from finding someone, just be aware of the lessons I learned so you don't have to go through it yourself.

When I found my first person to talk to it was because they had similar interests to me, but they also had similar issues. I thought I needed someone who understood what I was going through (and I did) but what I didn't need was someone who was going through it *right now*. What I thought was a mutually beneficial relationship based on openness, in the end, was more of a symbiosis (*Weeee aaaaaare DEPRESSSSSION* for any Venom fans out there). We talked about our issues, which felt good and right and helpful at the time, but we often dragged each other further and further away from the light. I chose someone who was *too much* like me. Like any good relationship, what I should have looked for was someone with the skills I lacked; someone to oppose my downsides, not match them.

What I should have been looking for was a person who was strong, open, a listener, but who didn't have their own Down Days. Because when they did, and I did too, we fed each other. Their problems became my problems. Perhaps we understood a little *too* well. And neither of us were capable of distancing ourselves from not only our own issues, but those of the other person. Spiral, spiral. We were NOT good for each other.

Thus, the parable of the mistake has been passed on.

How you find your confidant is up to you. For some people, their parents are the best match. For some, it's their partner. You might have the confidence to go straight to the doctor. I envy you. I couldn't have done that. Go talk to the person who fulfils *your* needs (and, as I mentioned above, who has the things that you lack) because on your Down Days you're vulnerable, and you have to concentrate on what you need at that very moment.

Afterward, make it up to them. Thank them, at least. Tell them it helped. Ask if they're ok.

"Thank you. That really helped. Are you alright?"

Just like that. Because those words are the difference between being an emotional leech and a friend who needs help. Having been around other depressives, I've seen both kinds. Ask if it's ok to talk openly, first, and check in afterwards. A few words can maintain that relationship, and make sure that the person you care about isn't being affected by your depression, too.

What if there isn't anyone?

THIS IS THE toughy. Not everyone has people around. It seems like a crazy thing to say in a world where contacting people is so easy, but what if there's no one to contact?

Depression can spiral. When it hit me, it hit hard. As I crumpled under the weight of everything that I'd been holding in, I thought that it had come all at once. But in truth it's a slower downward slope. As I said before, you're not always thinking straight, you don't always know that you're not thinking straight and, sometimes, your depression has causes which haven't just affected you short-term, but have been key in the shaping of your personality. That's something completely out of your control, and a very hard habit to change (although by no means impossible).

For some people I've known (and for myself) the crushing effects of low self-esteem are pretty important. It can be a parent being generally horrible, bullying in school, a history of partners with abusive behaviour, or any number of other things. In some terrible cases, it's a combination of all of those. What that sometimes develops is a self-destructive personality. Let's use body image as a starting point.

[Apologies for the bullet points, I know they're a bit formal].

- You have been told for years that you are fat by people who don't know better
- Your coping mechanism is eating (for some it's alcohol or drugs or smoking)
- So, you eat to make you feel better in the short term. But minutes after you've eaten half a cheesecake (I've done this and then some), you feel so very guilty that it dips you even lower so…
- You go eat something

This kind of compulsion isn't as easy to get rid of as "put the fork down". Because, believe me, when you feel so low, you'll do anything you can for just a few moments of feeling better. Again, You Number One is making themselves feel better with a cupcake and You Number Two is screaming, unheard, from a distance. It also doesn't help that food-that-is-bad-for-you is way easier to get hold of, and far tastier, than food-that-is-good-for-you.

But sometimes it isn't as easy as that little cycle, because people are complicated creatures and we don't fit into categories and lists as well as some would like.

Now, say you've eaten and you're feeling guilty and low. You have that history of horrible partners which has left you emotionally susceptible. You crave positive attention because you never had enough of it in healthy amounts. So, you're feeling down and someone of your preferred sexual orientation gives you a little attention. This can be a compliment, a sextual message, anything. Someone out there is giving you attention in your lowest moment. What do you do? You grab it with both hands and hold on. You're more inclined to throw yourself on that person without thinking. The thing is, not everyone is very nice. Some people just like to toy with others and seek out those who are already in a vulnerable state to get what they want. And you're so eager that you give it to them for the single moment of human contact that it gives you.

The problem? They don't actually care.

Once the deed is done, they disappear to find a new victim, leaving you alone again. Cast aside again. Used again. And, with no-one around to talk to or get some positive feedback from, you reach for the second half of that cheesecake.

This theory of mine (with no basis in science. This is just how it can be) comes out looking like a Mobius strip:

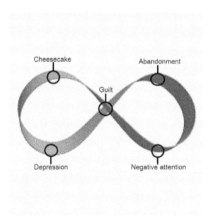

[How's that for a terribly executed piece of Microsoft Paint?]

You see what I mean? It's not just a vicious cycle. The thing is the damned *sign for infinity*! No wonder it's so hard to break free of it.

I have no answers for how you break out of this one. Not a clue. That's your counsellor/psychiatrist's speciality. But can you see, The Interested, how easily a person can be drawn into that infinite loop?

I could use that same picture to describe why you "need" a cup of coffee. The difference is that one of those pictures leaves someone on the brink of desolation, the other is something you laugh about with your friends despite the fact dependency on caffeine is still pretty bad (but socially accepted, so it's ok).

Why now?

[Coming back to read this chapter, I feel like a warning is in order. This gets a bit ranty. I apologise.]

IT SEEMS THAT depression is rife, doesn't it? You hear so many stories (usually of "celebs" *vomit* because they're the only ones who count, apparently) about people committing suicide, statistics pour out of newspapers and the TV screen at you. Depression is on the rise. The end is nigh. Cthulhu rises!

Why *is* that?

I don't have an answer. I did warn you that I won't be throwing psychobabble or stats at you. But the thought came to me when I overheard a conversation between two elderly people in the pub. Two old men, who sit at the same spot each day, as far as I can tell. They are about 300 years old. They have danced in the flame of immortality. To hear them speak, they have single-handedly won every war since

Tudor times. Their lives are a constant barrage of hardship overcome by spit and willpower. I'm happy for them. I really am. But what they were talking about the other day had me listening in even more intently than usual. (I eavesdrop. It's an author thing, leave me alone). One of them said something along the lines of:

"How come young folks these days are all depressed? We went through a world war and never got depressed. They're all soft."

I've heard this argument before. You probably have, too. And I have a bullshit theory that has no basis in science at all.

We are a generation built on awareness. 'Back in the day,' television was something the Nazis used to show how cool their gadgets were. There wasn't even anything transmitted during the Second World War. Compare that to today, where every murder, every act of terrorism, every war is constantly streamed into our expectant faces through the TV, the newspapers and the internet, flooding our social media in the form of Facebook posts and Tweets. Hell, the latest war in Afghanistan literally has a kill-streak counter. For every British soldier who falls in the line of duty, the news channels hear a little *ping* and they hyena that tragedy for days on end. Utterly putrid.

Tragedy isn't just in printed stories like the old days, but in high definition, full-colour, and surround sound. It's like that scene from A Clockwork Orange where Alex is forced to take in atrocities while listening to his favourite Beethoven movement. We can't look away because the internet is shiny and helps us keep in touch and find things out and not get lost and play Pokémon Go (Team Instinct for the win!). Then, of course, it's all our fault.

Care more.

Do more.

Take responsibility.

While being assured there's nothing we can do, that we're essentially doomed, we're also told that we're the only ones who can fix the planet. We're given responsibility (nay, blame!) but no power. Everything is broken. We know more now than ever before. It's no wonder depression is everywhere. Wherever you go, the politicians and bigots are waiting for you. For every hand you shake, there's a Westboro Baptist Church. For every door you hold open, there's a madman mowing down innocents in a school.

For some people, these things happen elsewhere and elsewhen. For those of my generation and mind-set, they're right there in your face and screaming. How am I supposed to ignore it? How am I supposed to plod along in my mundane life when suit-wearing shiny-faced automatons are sowing tragedy and reaping money?

And that's a major problem for me, I think. Because for all my practicality and common sense (two skills I *do* have) I can't help but look around me and see desolation on the horizon. I'm the kind of person who has hope for the future, who thinks that humankind has such potential for brilliance on the small scale, but when the people in control try to think bigger, they get brain freeze. Perhaps this is because I was raised on Roddenberry (the optimistic Star Trek creator, for those who aren't familiar). I want to live to see people traverse the void of space. I want to see everyone admit that a difference of religion is just about different versions of the same book, like discussing which version of Bladerunner is the best. Talk about it over a cuppa like a normal person and stop killing each other.

If you, Man-in-the-pub, can watch the planet fall apart without getting depressed, then I think you, sir, are the one with a problem. If anything, depression is the only option. I'm amazed the numbers aren't higher.

[This rant has been interrupted on behalf of the British Stiff Upper Lip who won't hold with that sort of thing].

Being Bold

A T FIRST, I tried not to tell people that I have depression. Saying you have depression has become an admission of guilt. It's seen as weakness of character. I'll be damned if I'm going to be beaten by a function of my brain.

Of course, then comes the time when it pops up in conversation. Some folks like to lead with it. I've met these people, and I can say without worrying that this is not cool. No person wants someone they barely know, or have never met before, coming up to them and starting the conversation with something resembling:

(Apologies in advance to the lovely Tims out there)

"Hello, I'm Tim and I have the occasional urge to end it all."

What a douche bag. What you're doing there Not-Nice-Tims-of-the-world is not only harming your own social interactions, but the interactions of Those Like You. Because this kind of thing still has a social stigma attached. It shouldn't, but it does. And that means, as sufferers (I'm using that term because that's how it feels) of Down Days in this transition period where we're trying to make it less taboo, you're damaging our cause.

The first way you're doing this is by making people think that Those Like Us are defined by their illness. People already do this without our help.

"Oh, have you heard he's gone off the deep end, again?"

"Who?"

"Craig. Depression Craig."

That's how people see others, as a name and a qualifier. I'll be damned if mine is going to be that one. I'd prefer "Craig the arsehole." And I'm sure you don't want to be known as "Sarah who took the overdose," or "Mark who hears voices," (also known as Crazy Mark). Although I'm talking about my own experiences of depression, we're also fighting a larger battle here, one for every person with mental health issues who gets along just fine. Psychopathy, for instance, isn't all about being a *ree* *ree* *ree* Psycho (that's my shower-stabbing-sound, in case you were wondering).

For instance, I rate pretty high on the psychopath scale, and yet have never hurt a single person (or one in a relationship for that matter. PUNS!) or animal in my life. I'm usually the first weighing in with First Aid, in fact. I also hear voices all the time. So do you, The Interested. Every time you look in the mirror and think "I look fat," you're hearing a negative voice in your head. It doesn't have to be telling you that space aliens have vulnerabilities to tinfoil hats, to be a voice. Some people have positive voices that tell them they look amazing, that everyone loves them, that their opinion matters more than everyone else. That's exactly the same schizophrenic condition, but there's no stigma attached to it. These people become Kardashians or Trumps, and by the time we realise that they're completely bonkers, they're running the country. And you're worried about Chris, working in your local shop, having a bit of OCD?

Anyway, I find the best way to mention that I have depression comes at a similar time that you should mention you have an allergy. Someone presents you with a peanut, and it's probably best to let them know that your face will explode. In the same way, when someone mentions depression and is either mis-informed or wants to genuinely discuss the topic, I weigh in. I point out that the person they've been talking to all night has depression. If they're being an arse, I shut them down. If they're genuinely interested then I try to convey some of the things you've been reading about here while grinning like a loon and edging toward the knife drawer, just to see what they'll do (Kidding! *Mostly*).

My point for Those Like Me is that you should be no more embarrassed about your depression than you should about being lactose intolerant. On the one hand, no one wants you running amok wielding a severed head in a Hitchcock-fuelled rampage, just like no-one wants you farting anthrax after eating some brie. But they're about to see that mental health isn't like that. Because you're brave and confident and you're about to explain it to them.

Understanding and education is more useful to us than anything else you can come up with. In a few decades, when the stigma has diminished, people won't know our names, but we'll have been there, fixing things, person-by-person, spreading the word.

"Leave me alone, I'm lonely."

—P!nk

Make up your mind

ONE OF THE most regular problems I suffer from is a lack of peace. When I'm on a Down Day, I really can't handle new information. I can't handle conversation. I like to be left alone. I'm not sure whether this has something to do with being an only child. (Where my introverts at? You get me, right?). I like peace, and quiet. Even on an Up Day I'd rather go for a walk in the sun on my own most of the time. It gives me time to be quiet and think and philosophise and, usually, come up with new story ideas. But it becomes especially true when I'm on a Down Day. It becomes a *need*. The sound of another person's voice, no matter who it is, just grates on me.

Now here comes the real kick in the pants because, when I'm on one of those Down Days, I don't always want to be alone. I want to be quiet, but not on my own. Being alone makes me worse. It's how I tend to end up because peace and company don't mix easily. It's one of the hardest things in the world to find someone who will suffer me being down and still want to sit right there. Other people need stimulation, obviously. So, finding someone who's willing to not watch TV or talk or anything at all but sit with me is almost impossible.

I'm not suggesting that this is somehow their fault. I'd be bored as hell, too, if I were them. What I am suggesting is that someone needs to invent a contraption to fix this huge depressive dilemma. Like, whenever you're ready, guys.

Seriously.

Any time, now.

Am I selfish?

ANOTHER THING WE'RE taught by our mummies and daddies when we're wee little bairns (not sure why the Scottish lilt, there) is to always put other people first. That's what I was taught, anyway. Be kind, be compassionate, be supportive of other people. Not for reward, but because that's just how it's done. I still believe that, if everyone could just be a little nicer, the world might sort itself out.

However, that kind of hardwired thinking has caused me some problems on my Down Days, and also in times when I've felt one coming on. Because, as I may have mentioned before, while putting other people ahead of yourself can be dangerous behaviour for anyone, that's especially true for a depressive.

You're at a party. It's been organised for months. You can't not go. Let's say it's God's birthday, or something. He'd be really pissed if you bailed and a divine smiting is something you want to avoid. Anyway, you *have* to go.

Except, it's a Down Day. Still, you get ready and head out. While you're there, you're a bit subdued, obviously. You hog a corner, drinking your beverage of choice quietly, content to let the party happen around you. But then the music is grating, the people won't stop moving around, their voices are like needles.

It's time to go.

Except, they don't want you to leave. The other deities are your friends (apparently, you're friends with God, like, on a social scale. I didn't think this analogy through very much) and they want you around. That's sweet of them, but what I'd need in that moment is to get the hell out, and probably in a rush because I always leave these things until the very last minute. I never learn. And so, with a fixed grin, I would make my apologies and leave. I've left them probably complaining about what a misery I am, and that will plague me for a while.

But does getting out when the anxiety rises and the world gets too much make us selfish?

Possibly. I guess it depends if you think a diabetic is selfish for excusing themselves to take their insulin, or a new mother is selfish for breastfeeding her child (if you think that breastfeeding in public is shameful, get the hell out). Is it selfish to go pee?

I've had this several times in the past so I can say with certainty that, at that moment, I need fresh air and peace and to be left alone. When I step out it's usually because the anxiety is getting to me. What I *think* would be more of a fun-killer is if I dropped to my knees in the middle of the dancefloor and started to have a panic attack.

Oh yeah, now the party's really getting started. *Woop woop*!

I wish people would just let me go. I really *need* to go. The only other option is to just sneak out, but that's so rude. Rudeness causes more anxiety. There's no winning here, I don't think.

It's what I was talking about with Plath's poem, *Tulips*. Laid in a hospital bed, she isn't thinking about her husband and children at home without her, she isn't even thinking about being ill, really. She's thinking how damned peaceful it is to be left alone, to the point that being ill enough to be in hospital is actually preferable.

I get that, Sylvia. I totally get it.

So, by extension, I get how people can sometimes make themselves ill on purpose. People who self-harm to the point of hospitalisation, for instance. I know why they do that. I get it. When the anxiety or depression builds up inside you like that, there's no outlet.

Crying expresses sadness, but it doesn't necessarily treat anxiety. You could scream out loud, and sometimes it works and sometimes it doesn't. Because what you're trying to do is fix a psychological issue with a physical action. Yes, we feel anxiety in the physical sense (mine is that brick sitting right under my diaphragm) but it doesn't come from there. There's no way to open a little tap in your head to let the steam out (a serious oversight in the design of humans, if you ask me). With nothing but raging frustration and the drowning sensation of losing control of yourself as you're dragged down into an anxious abyss, what can you do about it? People cut themselves, they take too many pills. These aren't the actions of a suicidal person, necessarily. But that doesn't mean they don't mean it, either. There's a reason it's called a "cry for help." It's because there's nothing else out there for us.

[What I forgot to mention here is that the problem with a "cry for help" of course, is that it has become synonymous (big word. Must have been reading dictionary toilet paper again) with "attention seeking" or "crying wolf." Another of the many social stigmas that need to change. Because yes, it is a cry for help. That means that *someone needs to give some!*]

I finally plucked up the courage to go to my doctor and ask for counselling. What about those poor souls who never get there? Or the ones who sit at home with the crushing sense of futility because they've been to the doctors before and have been ignored or discharged from input because they don't *score enough*?

When I had my counselling, because I didn't completely lose my shit and smash up the office or try to hang myself from the curtain rail right in front of her by the time I'd had three sessions, I wasn't allowed to have more. How mad is that? I'd put down on my assessment that I was having suicidal thoughts. However, I wasn't bringing in the roadkill from outside and calling it Clarence so, apparently, that doesn't score high enough to get consistent help.

This is because, when it boils right down to it, if there's no physical evidence of you being ill, the people who make healthcare legislation in this country don't think there's anything wrong. So, what do we do? We commit a cry for help. We *give them* a damned physical symptom. And then they berate us for seeking attention.

Lose-lose, my friends.

And do you know the *really* sad thing about this? The thing that's even worse, in my perspective, than me sitting there awe-struck by the stupidity of it? My counsellor agreed. She seemed so saddened by the fact that she had to break it to me. She actually apologised for the system's stupidity. I felt bad for her. Because, it may affect my life, but she gets to see more people like me every day who are not just slipping through the net, but for whom the net doesn't even exist. How soul crushing that must be for someone who genuinely cares.

"Whenever I'm feeling down after losing a battle, I think, "at least I've still got my shorts!"

—Youngster, Pokémon Red/Blue

Sometimes there's just no winning

F OR ALL OF the positive memes you'll find on Pinterest and Facebook about holding in there and living your dreams and remembering that you're stardust, some days there's just nothing you can do. It's going to be rubbish today. There's no positivity in you. No one else can pick you up.

I had one of those days yesterday. Everything just fell apart. I got bad news by phone and mail and facial delivery (someone told me), all about different things. My brain, helpful as it is, just went *blart* and decided that enough was enough. So, yesterday was not a productive day.

There are days like those often in life. But Those Like Me don't get to hit refresh after the Error 404 message. It sticks around. And there's nothing you can do about it. Yesterday was cancelled, basically. I would get nothing done because that knot I mentioned before was just too damned distracting. I tried reading, I listened to my music, I worked on my next novel (for all of ten minutes then felt bad about not doing more), and nothing worked.

Of course, when I'm like that, I'm a bit all over the place. When I'm not on a Down Day, I'm pretty focussed. I sometimes forget to eat and drink for a whole day if I'm in the zone with some project or other. But yesterday's Down Day just had me wandering back and forth between failed distractions, not really taking any of them in. It was hellish. I felt almost incorporeal; a wandering shade that passes through everything it touches. My mind was so full of static that I couldn't even remember getting from one room to the next. I was just there.

Of course, those around you know what's going on. You're hauntingly quiet, for instance. They care, and so they ask if you're alright. You just say yes, because sometimes explanations fail you. Because sometimes, when you're floating through one of those days, trying to come up with a reason for it seems like picking a staring contest with the Eye of Sauron.

Another trial

S O, AS I mentioned before, I have recently left a job which was not only making me miserable, but also quite ill. Anyway, I've taken a huge plunge in walking out of that place for the sake of my mental health. However, my positive choice has left me in a negative place. I'm without a job, so without any income. I've never been without a job before. Not since I started working at sixteen years old. This is not good.

And today I have another hit to both pride and patience. Today I have to sign up for Jobseeker's Allowance until I can find work. For someone who has always earned their own money through hard work and perseverance, it's a real kick to my stubborn pride that I have to do this. But, that's not what's causing the anxiety today. What I'm really worried about is The Conversation.

For Those Like Me, The Conversation happens more often than The Interested might think. There is no way to light up the Bat-signal and inform everyone at once that I have mental health issues. There's no insignia to wear and no tattoo on my forehead (thank God). Which means, every time we come across a new person who doesn't know us, but who needs to know about our condition, we have to tell our story all over again. I don't tend to revel in that, as I'm sure you can imagine.

So today I get to sit across from a person that probably thinks I'm a lazy shit who doesn't want to work, and explain to them why I can't return to the very profession that I have sixteen years of experience in due to the fact that it would probably kill me.

The Joy!

I'll return to this chapter later, I think, once the interview is over, and let you know how it went. Cross your fingers.

[Some time later...]

THAT ACTUALLY WASN'T so bad. In fact, it was quite interesting, in some ways. The lady who did my interview wasn't a Balrog, as I expected her to be. Apart from dismissing all the writing experience on my CV as "not counting," I think it went pretty smoothly. She even took my explanation of why I couldn't return to my previous profession quite coolly, in an almost disinterested way. I guess she's heard it all, in her line of work. The main hurdle was the anxiety.

As usually happens when I'm anxious about something, I arrived super early. I do this all the time. It weighs on my mind so much, making me jittery and I start wandering around my house looking for things to distract me. When that fails, I end up setting off super early, making all kinds of excuses as to why I should. Maybe the traffic will be horrendous. Maybe I'll get lost (in my own home town? Yeah, right). I don't think I'm even conscious of it most of the time. But still, I arrived forty minutes early. I'd also taken everything I could possibly need, and more. With a pile of papers on my person, it turned out that I only needed my driver's licence and passport. Luckily, the bag I took with me also had room for a book so, while I was waiting for my appointment slot, I could read. That helped the anxiety a little. That brick-heart feeling was still there but the book distracted me enough that it didn't get worse.

So, despite the knock to my pride, I think I'd call that a success. I felt exhausted when I got home, but that's just the adrenaline, I guess.

Not-quite-Down Days

I'M HAVING ONE of those days where I don't really know what to do with myself. I have a stack of work to do with two novels, a few articles to write and even some editing for other people's books (which is way more fun than it should be), but I just can't bring myself to do it. I woke up with a crushing headache this morning, kicking the day off to a great start. Then the anxiety was there again. I still haven't found a job [this is only a month after leaving work, so hardly an age] and it's starting to worry me. I've applied for so many different posts, it's crazy. Anything at all. All coming to nothing so far.

The writing that I'm filling my time with seems to be going well. This book, for instance, is turning out longer than I anticipated. I'm still not sure if it's relevant to you out there, or if I'm waffling on pointlessly, but I'm still doing it. It seems to have shifted into an almost diary-like creature that I wasn't anticipating, but I think that might work alright. The point was to show you all examples of what it's like to live with depression, right? I guess anecdotes will do that best. Apparently my sub-conscious knew that before I did. Typical.

Anyway, back to today.

So, it's one of those days. I've been like a stepped-on-cat all day. Jumpy, jittery. Staying in is giving me cabin fever. Going out seems pointless without somewhere to go. I'm pretty sure my friends and family will be getting sick of me by now so I'm trying to keep it as much to myself as humanly possible. And, more annoying than anything, while this book is going well, my fiction writing is going slooooooooow. I have all these ideas but they just aren't coming out right. Not in a "this writing is bad" way, because that's how I write anyway (he joked while being deathly serious), I mean in a brain-to-finger co-ordination kind of way. It seems crazy, I know, because I'm typing this instead, but this is different somehow. Maybe it comes from a different part of my brain. I'm basically typing what my internal monologue would be saying anyway, which is very different from writing a philosophical cyberpunk novella with non-binary characters, I suppose. An odd thing, the brain.

So, today is one of those days where I write a few words, get up and walk around, realise there's nothing to see, and come to sit back down again. Then I check Twitter for the millionth time, realise there's nothing new there either, and go back to writing. The whole day has been filled with variations on this theme.

But I don't feel down as such. This isn't one of my

special cocoon-style days. Me Number One and Me Number Two are still there. It just feels like they might be speaking in an accent that the other can't understand. I know it's the same language, but something is different enough that they just can't get along.

Sod it. I'm going to sign off and start again tomorrow.

"Victims, aren't we all?"
—Eric Draven, *The Crow*

Burden

THE FACT IS, whether we like it or not, having depression or other mental health issues is seen as unnatural, abnormal, and is generally frowned upon. This is most applicable to people with no empathy for their fellow humans, and we are *drowning* in those people. I can see where they're coming from, of course. On an evolutionary level if someone can't get along on their own then they shouldn't be around. If I had a Down Day on the Serengeti back when we were still monkeys and a lion was wandering by, I'd be eaten first. The rest of the Australopithecus would run up their tree hooting and hollering while I opened my arms to the approaching wall of teeth, humming a song by The Smiths (crossing the streams there, sorry).

However, here's the thing: we're not monkeys anymore. We're supposed to be better than that. Seeing people with mental health issues as a burden is the same as seeing someone with any physical illness as a burden. You just can't see what we have on a scan. And that's what confuses people. In a world where everything is available and in-your-face, from the over sexualisation of media to blood-spurting gore in our movies and the news ramming negativity into our heads at every turn without any reproach, there should be something on that scan, something to see. That's how the world works, isn't it?

No, it bloody isn't.

Some things are unknown, or at least beyond our understanding. For a species who has a little organ on our large intestine which does nothing more than try to kill us at random intervals, you'd think we'd be a little more open to the quirks and intricacies of our bodies and minds.

Rather than being seen as the lovable scamps that we are, Those Like Me are seen as a burden, instead.

The worst part? We *know* it, because we live in that society too and we've been brought up surrounded by the same beliefs. Even for someone like myself who thinks it's deplorable how Those Like Me are so often misunderstood, I still feel like a burden while trying to convince myself that I shouldn't have to feel that way.

I'm not a burden.

Alright, I've had to walk out of a job in healthcare due to my illness and as I sit writing this, I have no job. But I've worked for the National Health Service for *sixteen years*. I started work at sixteen years old and I've worked every day since then. In that time, I've written and published a number of books, completed two degrees (with a 2:2 and a 2:1 result, if you're interested) and paid my taxes like an upstanding citizen. I've helped run conventions, and even events for the theatre in my home town. I swear to whatever deity you hold dear; I've helped an old lady across the street. I've bloody saved lives. How exactly am I a burden?

Other depressives I know are some of the funniest, most creative and caring people I've ever met; people who I hold dear. I've also come across people who abuse others in the street for the fun of it, or abuse children, or run a system of government which is tearing the country apart due to blatant, sweaty-faced greed. Who is the most burdensome to society? That's rhetorical, but feel free to shout it out loud anyway.

They are!

(Deep breath aaaaaand calm).

Recently, as you might know, a certain Tory MP [I was going to use her name but won't reward her stupidity with the google searches] suggested that people with mental health issues should wear coloured wristbands so that emergency workers can know about our issues on sight. Why stop there? I'll just hop over to my local vet and get a GPS chip. Hey, everyone has cool tattoos, right? I'll have a barcode on my wrist encoded with my mental health history to save people the time of actually talking to me.

Insert a slow, sarcastic clap

This is what we contend with; people so far out of touch with the subjects they're trying to have a strong opinion on that they come up with outlandish suggestions. That person is an MP in our ruling government [at time of writing that was true but hopefully it won't be as you read this. Sorry, politics, I know. I shouldn't get into it here]. What if that idea had stuck? If you've ever seen an episode of *The Thick*

Of It, you'll see how these ideas come about. Except that show is supposed to be a comedy…and this is our lives.

And as well as the crushing emotional onslaught Those Like Me weave through every day, there's the fear. I'm afraid. I'm scared of what the next political idea will be, and that it *will* stick. I'm sometimes petrified at the thought that some quirk of my mind means I'll never be useful again. I thrive on doing things, creating things, working hard. What if people continue to ask me in job interviews why I left Nursing and I'm too honest to not say "I suffer from depression and the job was making me ill"? That's a huge cross on my interviewer's checklist. I'm scarred for life because I refuse to lie. I shouldn't have to. But if Those Like Me don't hide it, we might as well be wearing that wristband. Because the way our country works right now, 'admitting it' is enough to be blacklisted from society. You try getting a job when no-one "wants to have to deal with you."

And then they wonder why we hide, why so many of us don't have "normal" jobs, but sit outside society, scraping through by being authors or musicians, jewellery makers or artists. Why do you think the suicide rate among Creatives is so high? The drug addiction, the drinking. It's because society doesn't understand or want us, and so we take to our sheds and our studies, recording studios and hotel rooms, and do what we can to express ourselves when no one is listening.

I have no statistics for you, but I bet if you were to look into it, some of the most creative and influential artists of history have suffered with Down Days. I don't count myself among them, because I'm not a douchebag, but think about it:

- Amy Winehouse – A flame of talent snuffed out by a torrent of self-destruction.
- Robin Williams – Brought joy to every person he touched. Every one. Except himself.
- Ernest Hemingway – Pulitzer and Nobel prize winner. Ended it all with a shotgun.
- And, of course, Sylvia Plath, who remains a singular voice for Those-Like-Me.

And that's without mentioning those who didn't commit suicide but who struggled with any number of addictions to take the pain away. I may be over-simplifying, but I think you see my point.

It's a long, black night that we're driving through. We've come a long way already, since women who had children outside of wedlock were thrown in asylums with dangerous criminal lunatics. Maybe one day in the future, if we keep working at it, we'll stop being seen as a burden to society and stop having to hide away just to get some semblance of a life.

Holiday

I'VE JUST BEEN on holiday. Luckily, we'd paid for it before I walked out of my job and so we could still go. One week in the sun. It was glorious and the food was great and there was plenty of wine. Then there were the Down Days, because Down Days don't care if I'm happy and content and relaxed. It's me they hate specifically, not my current mood or the proximity of a beach.

We were maybe four days into the holiday when the Down Day arrived. I woke up already feeling it and knew where it was headed. But it wasn't the usual kind. This was a different breed which comes to me a little less often, but is always perfectly timed for destruction. The "twitchy" kind.

These twitches wait for the perfect moment to strike; when I can't get access to the internet, when my laptop is broken, or sometimes when I just have too much to do. They wait until the very moment when I can't be productive and then they won't let me forget about it.

It can be defined as a "I need to move/work" compulsion, I guess. I *have* to do something. I can try to tell myself to be patient, there's nothing to be done, the laptop will be fixed tomorrow, or *you're in another bloody country so chill out*. But the world is moving too fast and I can feel it spinning under my feet, and I can't switch off. There's a flurry of life to pay attention to and my mind won't focus on one aspect of it for more than a second. I'm in the middle of a maelstrom of my life and the very fact that, right now, I can't do a damned thing about it is what makes the twitchiness so perfectly shitty.

You see, not all Down Days are really 'down', as such. Sometimes, I flip the other way. I had one of these periods while I was on holiday. In truth, it ate the last three days. It ruined everything I'd been looking forward to, which only made the come down from this thought-high all the worse.

I'm the equivalent of the kid smacked off his face on too much fizzy pop and sherbet or maybe Daffy Duck with his tail on fire, running around the walls and bouncing back and forth on his head when I think of the books I have to write, the paperwork I have to do, setting up that blog, signing the contract for my new book and there's a stack of washing to do when we get home and it feels terrible because the whole time I can't stop thinking about how much time I'm wasting how much there is to do I'm going to die one day and I'll have all this work still to do and people can tell, my wife can tell, and that means I'm ruining it for her, too, because now she's worried about me and wants to help and so she's talking to me about it and I can't listen properly because there's too much noise in my head and she's just making it worse but don't leave me alone because I'm spinning and I don't know what to do and I can feel the migraine pulsing behind my left eye and that means I'm in for a long, dark lie down which will make finding a distraction so much worse and *aaaaaaarrrgh!*

Sounds like fun, right?

Sometimes the breathing trick works for this, 4-7-8, and sometimes I need to find something, one thing, to focus on and hold it. This time it was like Slimer dodging Stantz's proton beam. There was no catching the ugly little spud. I had a notebook with me, and my phone, and so did everything I could to get down whatever was in my head, but it just didn't work.

And now we're back home and all I can think about is how I ruined the last few days of that holiday, maybe the last holiday we'll have in a long time, by being a bloody weirdo. It's so frustrating I could scream. But I'm back, and there are chapters to write; an exorcism of the literary kind.

Let there be words.

Existential Crisis

I'M PRETTY SURE that's what's going on with me right now. Or maybe I'm having a mid-life crisis early. Or maybe it's just a regular crisis. Sorry for repeating myself, but I like to be busy, to have a function, to be working toward something. I hate sitting down and doing nothing. Writing this book hasn't really quenched the thirst because it's something deeper that I need. It isn't a project, but definition that I seek. Categories are horrible things that were once useful tools but which have taken over our world so that we can't exist without knowing which one we fit into. Categories are basically Skynet. And, right now, I have no category. Part of me would love to be totally alternative about this and start wearing my disenfranchisement like a badge of honour but, you know what? A category is a trampoline under the slippery tree of life. I need to know what I am because I don't have much else.

And so, I'm living in a society which has asked me from

the age that I learned to speak, "what do you want to be when you grow up?", and then has forced me to think about it every day of my life like it's all that I'm worth. Except now…I don't know. I'm uncategorisable (made that word up as well. Don't care). I am *that* grown up, and I'm not Spider-man yet. How the hell do I deal with that?

You're right, I could get a job stacking shelves or scrubbing the putrid humanity stains from toilets to pay my bills, and I have done so in the past. Well, I've managed better than those, thank Cthulhu. I now have a post as a teaching assistant in a college, helping kids (I'm an old man now, so that's how I see them) with barriers to learning to get where they need to be.

Rewarding, right? Yes.

Soul destroying? That too.

Because this job has shown me what I was happily hiding from the last few months that this books spans. I should be doing more with myself, and I'm not. I've worked hard to get my two degrees and the years of writing and real-life experience. I should be flying. I should be bloody *soaring*. That's what they told me would happen in school. They promised. But the reality hiding behind these lies has not only brought me crashing down but stamped on my wings, cut them off and thrown them away.

This thing that I live with has made a dodo of me, leaving me staring up at albatrosses, wanting desperately to join them and knowing deep down in my soul that I wouldn't last a second in the sky. You and me, we have potential. That's the strength in humans. It always has been. We change year to year, day to day, second to bloody second.

I'm not being very articulate here. What's my point? Possibly, that I don't have a plan, or even an inkling of an idea or where I'm headed. I'm tortured by it. That *need* to be something, to do something worth doing so that I can one day look back and perhaps convince myself for a second that I haven't wasted a lifetime.

Instead, I'm staring up from a pebbly beach and the humans are arriving. I think I'll go make friends and see how that goes…

Katabasis

THAT'S A COOL word, isn't it? Do you know what it means? If you just answered yes, can you please stop being so intelligent? It makes me look bad. I had no idea what it was.

I came across *katabasis* completely by accident when I was researching for one of my stories. But it's absolutely brilliant!

It's an ancient Greek word, in case you're interested. It came to be a metaphor for a lot of things but the important meaning for us is what we'll call The Downward Journey. You've probably heard of Hercules, yes? Muscley guy, looks like Kevin Sorbo, did some impressive things like slaying monsters or, occasionally, capturing them. He also mucked out the Augean stables, which means that he had to clean up the shit of a thousand cattle in a single day. That one I can relate to in particular. But katabasis has nothing to do with that.

Hercules did some other stuff (like fighting Xena Warrior Princess) but also, he had to go down to the underworld to rescue *history history myths and legends, blah blah*. So, he went to the underworld, and returned. That was an incredible feat, something that no one was supposed to be capable of. He literally went to hell and back (I wonder if that's where the saying comes from). Anyway, *katabasis* is interesting as a word and a concept because it aptly describes exactly what Those Like Me go through all the time. We travel in our minds (which we've established is just as powerful as any physical journey) not only to hell, but somewhere far worse.

Which is scarier? When you're watching a horror movie and the evil creature is spewing gore and dancing in the spotlight, or when you never really see it properly and your mind has to fill in the blanks? *Saw* is gory and gross, but when the camera pans away from Norman Bates shower-murdering of Mary in *Psycho* you have to imagine the horror yourself. That means your imagination picks whatever is scariest for you, personally, and fills in the blanks with it.

So, Hercules went to Hell. But what Those Like Me do is create our own hells. Not in a conscious way, obviously, but nothing can compare to the terror of an abyss that is filled with all the things that are specifically designed for you by the one person who knows exactly how to push your buttons. You.

The important part of *katabasis* is that *Hercules made it out*. He came back. And that's why I'm taking the word as my personal mantra. Every time I'm down from now on, I'm going to start saying that word out loud. Say it with me friends!

Katabasis

I'm heading down now, but I'll be back up soon. Can I get an A-men!?

It also helps that it's a fun word to say, but I'm easily amused.

The End?

WHEN I STARTED writing this book, I had no grand plan. This wasn't supposed to be about a journey with a nice neat ending or some great epiphany about life. I'm still here, doing this, living with it and managing it and trying to learn. If you're looking for that particular ending, I could write until the day I die and still be without answers.

And so, as I officially run out of useful (run out implies I had some at some point) things to say, how *does* it end?

If I think about depression, I guess it doesn't end. We live with it. We learn to manage it in our own special way. On our Down Days, we ride it out, and every other day of our lives we grab what we can, and make the most of it. The question is whether you want to be defined by your condition. Is it all you can be? Are you going to be Jenny-who-has-depression, or just Jenny?

Talk of 'deserving' better is useless. Waiting for luck is useless. There's just life, and life is random and hard. But it has always been random and hard; since the dawn of time when the first Neanderthal stubbed his toe, his mate got eaten by a sabre-toothed tiger, then lightning set his hut on fire, and the first Down Day in history was created [I'm aware that sabre-toothed tigers probably didn't exist in line with Neanderthals, and they probably didn't live in huts, but just go with me on this, ok?].

The only way that I can see to get through it is to expect the worst, steel yourself for it, but remember to hope for the best. Because the thing that happens between those two points is where we live.

Surrounding yourself with people who don't drag you down, but make you feel good, goes a long way to helping with this. If that means going to your local geek meeting, library, art installation or writer's group, then do that. You're already ridiculously brave and determined to get to this point so you can *definitely* do it.

As far as I can tell, we only get one shot and I'll be damned if I'm going to waste it. I can only suggest that you do the same. Try. If it doesn't work, reset the counter and try again. The attempt means everything.

And, so, Those Like Me, I hope you've taken something from reading my ramblings. I hope that you perhaps feel a little less alone, and a little more understood. The Interested, I hope you've had an insight into what it's like to live with depression, how serious it is, and how debilitating. I hope that the next time you come across someone with depression, you'll feel more equipped to understand your friend/partner/loved one.

That's all from me.

P.S. If you were hoping for bad poetry, you're not getting any. I lost my nerve, alright? Go read some Plath instead.

PART 3:

In which it wasn't The End

Guess who's back

D AMN, THAT WAS a good signing off. I'm quite proud of that.

Now here I come to ruin it.

Hello, gentlefolk. I'm back. Although it seems only the turning of a page since we last spoke (see what I did there?), it's actually been about two years. Two long years since I laid Down Days to rest and tried to get on with whatever this thing called 'life' is.

Results have varied.

In terms of Down Days, I released the eBook for free on a blog of the same name, extending the blabbering each week. It went far better than I expected. I was contacted by such lovely people, literally the world over, who read and enjoyed my little book of drivel. It made me feel like a very lucky author, indeed. What was perhaps more profound for me, but in no way diminished the feedback that I'm so grateful for, were the people I *already* knew who also got in touch. I had private messages from so many family and friends, or even friends of friends, who just wanted to say thank you because they struggled with things as well, and felt a little less alone from reading Down Days.

Thank you! Can you imagine?

For me, this whole experience means the absolute world. It means that I've done the one thing that I set out to do. I helped. If it had been just one person, I'd have been happy. As it is, with all your kind words, I feel extremely lucky.

So why am I darkening on your doorstep once more? Why has the fateful figure who once took you on a wild adventure returned on your eleventy-first birthday to stir things up again?

Unfortunately, after a year of writing the Down Days blog, it got a bit much for me. I was trying to break away from reliving that old stuff. I was trying to get out of the headspace, to break through the cloud and look forward (the road goes ever on and on...).

I was trying desperately to redefine myself, to evolve into something new, the emotional Charizard to my depressed Charmander. That meant letting go of the blog. And so, I did. But I left it there, for anyone who wanted to read it. Until recently. As I write this it was just last month that the website had to close.

You see, not much has changed, really. My fiction writing still doesn't pay the bills. The day job that I'm in doesn't really help the depression at all. I'm still making ends meet each month in any way I can. The site was an expense that I couldn't afford. Of course, as soon as I announced that it would be closing, you lovely lot jumped in. I had offers to pay for the site left right and centre, because you're all fucking awesome. But it felt wrong, somehow. Part of me hates that my work has to be funded by others (my pride is something I'm still working on). Perhaps a part of me wanted to see it taken down, wanted to see the story die so that *I* could let it die, too. That was pretty selfish of me, in hindsight. Because they might be my experiences, but other people found them useful. And, since we last spoke, I've got pretty damned philosophical about things like this. I have to be the change that I want to see. What if this thing that I've written makes a difference to one random person out there? That's more than enough reason to keep it alive despite my discomfort.

Luckily, seconds after I announced the site closing and thanked everyone for their support, my publisher got in touch (I didn't talk about Inspired Quill before now. I don't like to go on about my books and such because it feels all lardy-dar). They wanted to publish Down Days. They didn't want to see it die either.

Well, shit.

So, here I am. As I write this, I've just finished my first read-through after two long years. Ain't gonna lie, folks, I cried. I cried like the first time I wrote it. But you didn't really expect me to do anything else, did you? And now, I'm going to add some stuff.

The "end" of Down Days was nothing of the sort. We all knew it wouldn't be, right? I'm still here, living day-to-day and learning to manage my depression all the time. I told you that it was a long-haul job. So, I'm going to talk a little more about what's changed, what hasn't, and give you something new that's hopefully worth reading. Or, you know, I'll write it and realise it's crap and then delete it and you'll never know any different.

Mwahahahaha.

[I did, in fact, write thousands of words after this. I then completely rewrote them three times as I tried to figure out what the hell to say. The problem was, I felt like I should have some knowledge to pass on by now. But, after a while, I remembered that this isn't that kind of book. So, I boiled it down to what you'll read next which is more in the spirit of Down Days...]

The only project worth
working on

I HAD TO, and *still* have to, work on myself.

You all remember the talks of medication, of counselling and therapy, of long discussions with family and friends. That's all awesome and useful and pays off in buckets, but what I really needed to do was get my own shit in order.

This is mostly because, when I have a Down Day, it's hard to hear my internal monologue, never mind other people. I've tried to get better at building reflexes to counteract the shitty ones that cause a Down Day. So that, even when I can't hear myself think, I go into self-care autopilot and just let it happen. It might sound nuts but it's not too bad. It kinda works. I still need to work on reducing the reaction time between down and reflexively stable (and, more importantly, safe). But it's just like training for anything else. I'm slowly, slowly getting better at it.

Doing all this shit on your own is a great burden, of course, and sometimes it can feel like I'm building the pyramids solo with nothing but paper straws and strawberry laces. That seems far too big a thing for me to handle, so I've tried to shift my perspective to change the scale that I'm working on. Basically, all I've done is change the metaphor that I use to describe what I'm dealing with. Because I realised that the way I'd been visualising it was part of my problem. The one thing that I've always been able to count on, my imagination, is one of the things trying to throttle me.

In the last two years I've tried to go from seeing myself stood at the foot of my problems, looking up at the unsurmountable task of working on myself (pyramid building), to seeing myself sat cross-legged and comfortably, upturning the Lego box of my psyche (remember the sound of it spilling out onto the carpet? Sheer joy) to pick through the bricks. That's much more manageable, you see? It's a bonkers thing but it helps me. This might not work or mean *anything* to you, of course. You have to find your own little tweaks to make.

But every little tweak, if it only helps me a little, still helps. And I'll take everything I can get.

I realised, while digging through everything that makes me tick (which you might remember from the earlier chapters), that *this* is what it's all about. For me, at least. The really important project isn't my next novel or poem. The only thing really worth working on is myself.

cue trippy astral music and monk humming

The Project

I COULD GET super philosophical with you, but I don't want to. Not here at least. A beverage and somewhere comfy to sit are needed for that kind of heavy thinking. I will advise that you read more philosophy and poetry for yourself, though, because these are the salves of the human soul. I won't hear anyone say any different. But, otherwise, it's the little steps that I've been taking that have shown the greatest improvement.

I can recognise a Down Day when it's coming, usually the day before it happens which is nice. I've actually had some pretty big epiphanies about how I tick and which parts I can control and which I can't. These epiphanies give me solace on good days, and mean absolutely nothing on the bad ones. Standard operating procedure, *amiright*?

I still have Down Days and weeks, but they tend to be fewer and shorter. I'm still not great at self-care. While I tend to give myself headspace, walk more when I need to get out and that kind of thing, I still suck at knowing when to take a day off. Especially when it comes to the writing because it's the thing I'm most passionate about (aside from cheesecake). But recognising that I'm crap at self-care is at least a start, right? I'm proud of the progress I've made. It's taken two long fucking years to get anywhere near this even keel feeling.

How have I done it? Who cares! We've always said that what works for me won't work for you. Also, this isn't a self-help book. In a nutshell, rather than a "this will change your life and you'll be a perfect human being" kind of way, I've gotten to this mid-ground by reading philosophy, watching Neil Degrasse Tyson videos like they're going out of fashion, and having long, hard sessions of self-reflection with nothing but a cup of tea and a window to stare out of (it helps the self-reflection bah-dum-tsch).

I've learned when to look at the little things and when to look at the big things. I switch between working on the little parts of myself, and knowing that on a cosmic scale nothing I do really matters. It isn't as depressing as it sounds. It's actually quite freeing. I can change my behaviour, the way I am around people and the effect I have. I can spread goodness that way. I can't change everyone else. And that's not my job. I have to embody the change that I want to see as much as I can, and that's the extent of it. My responsibility ends there.

I try to expect the worst but hope for the best as a kind of low-grade mantra. That works when it works and doesn't when it doesn't. But it's there and better than expecting the worst and…that's all.

I'm also working on that pride thing. The thing that shoots my writing career in the foot. I ask for help, now. I ask people to share my work, to talk about it with others if they've enjoyed it. That always felt cheeky, to me, but I'm getting over it. In an attempt to actually afford things like food, I've even started a Patreon page which has been surprisingly freeing. I get to share new work with people which helps me to get feedback and encouragement (sorely needed with my imposter syndrome) and (this still gets stuck in my throat a little) ask for help from them. And, you know what? Breaking that stupid barrier down in my head has paid off. I now have some lovely people not only beta reading my new stories and poetry but also helping me to afford travel and table costs for signings and conventions, too. Basically, dropping my pride has done wonders for my career. At least, it might. It's still early days. It only took me thirty-three years to figure out. :D

The Middle (Comes At The End)

A S I WRITE this, I'm actually in the middle of the biggest down period that I've had in a long time (bad timing, I know, but I want to be honest as always). Yes, two years later, I still get them. I've been struck with the worst case of "I'm useless" lately (you might have noticed I have a bit of a problem with that), which leads to the good old thought process:

Why does no one read my books? *It's because you're shit.* Why is it so hard to just get people to read a damned book? *Because they see you for what you are. Shit.* Why do I do this to myself? *Good question, dickhead. Why do you?* How do I have the audacity to write something like this? Who gives a shit? *Nooooo ooooooone.*

Mix that in with the feelings of loneliness and isolation that I get an awful lot, and I can make a rough-weave hessian sack for myself to jump inside and pull the drawstring. This is the famous sack of shit that people always talk about.

I've been crying (more than usual), my concentration is off again, and I'm floating through not really committing things to memory. It's driving me nuts. My anxiety through all of this is overwhelming. While I'm sat here, typing to you lot, I'm fine. I'm in a safe zone where I can stop to cry if I need to or close my eyes and breathe deeply. I can't do that at the day job, obviously. And to add insult to injury, I have to call into work all the time to say "yes, I'm still depressed" and try not to cry to my manager. Modern life, the one that causes a great deal of this for Those Like Us, really adds insult to injury.

I'm also back on medication. No, not *that* medication that stopped me writing and thinking straight. First, I'm on something just for anxiety; it helps to keep the heart palpitations on a down low, and keeps me from getting completely overwhelmed by day-to-day symptoms. That heavy feeling is still there in my chest, but it doesn't threaten to crawl up my throat and punch me in the face as often. The second is a brand new one which, as I write this, I've been taking a total of three days. As you can imagine, the jury is still out on it. If I see any of you at a future signing or out and about, I'll let you know how that one goes.

Why am I back on the meds? Because what I can usually shrug off in a few days or a week has lasted two months. And I'm tired. Those black thoughts have been creeping back in like ink in water, and I've been a little scared of myself. I needed help. Sometimes, you need to consult the team if you're going to make the project the best it can be, right? I'm glad I went and got some advice because I instantly felt better. And this new medication seems to be working pretty well for me. Just like doctors and counsellors, not all medications are made equal and we all need different things. It's fair to say that a little experimentation *with the help of your medical professional* can be a good idea.

This is just a blip, though. A sodding blip, but a blip none-the-less. Because, in general, I have this shit down pat. By the guttural eldritch screechings of mighty Cthulhu, I'm better.

Not Better, but better. And not every day, but in general.

After a couple of years of hard work, I'm finding myself more centralised on the spectrum between suicidal and ecstatic. It's a nice place to spend a little time and I'm spending more of it there than elsewhere. My perspective has shifted from trying to make myself HAPPY!!! to just maintaining a little balance in the emotional midground. I've gotten to a point in my life where I'm fine. Just fine. But you know the thing about fine? It's actually pretty good. Because when I'm super happy, all I do is worry that I'll lose it. And when I'm down, all I do is worry that I've already lost it (puns!). But when I'm in the warm, fuzzy, midground where I'm not struggling, not striving, just ticking over nicely, I'm actually my happiest (confusing, I know).

I am my life's biggest project. But it's ok. I'm getting there. Just like losing weight too fast is bad for you, I'm getting better at managing this thing slowly, healthily, with practice and time.

And it feels good.

The End (really this time)

I JUST WANT to thank you all for reading. I mean it. Close your eyes and imagine I'm sat in front of you, leaning in and looking you right in the eye (scary, I know).

Thank *you*, specifically you.

You have all made one of the worst, most petrifying times of my life something that I can look back on with a little less fear and self-loathing. Every time I have a Down Day, when I feel at my lowest, when I think that nothing I've ever written means anything or will ever mean anything, I think about this book. This little thing that no one was ever supposed to read. Your feedback, your lovely comments, everyone who has shared this story and allowed it to reach someone else who might need it. You've all done this. So, when you feel like you've never done anything worthwhile, either, think that you've changed *my* perspective. You've all taught me that being open and honest and sharing can be a really rewarding experience. Because there are others like us who appreciate it. They appreciate you. *I* appreciate you. You've helped me to get closer to that person that I want to be, and embody the change I want to see.

(Bloody hell, I'm crying again *eye roll*)

Anyway, that got a bit hot and heavy so let's all grab a tissue and take a deep breath. This is where I sign off, properly this time, and let you get back to working on your own project. For what it's worth, from someone you've likely never met, I can tell you with all certainty that *you can do it*.

Because despite all the things that make us different, we're the same, you and I. And if a damned dirty ape like me can learn to manage this and get by just fine, then you can too.

Be good to each other. We're all we've got.

Dear Reader

Thank you for reading *Down Days*. If you enjoyed this book (or even if you didn't) please visit the site where you purchased it and write a brief review. Your feedback is important to both me and my publisher, and it will help other readers decide whether to read the book, too.

About the Author

Beginning his career with short stories in 2008, Craig's tales have graced the pages of the British Fantasy Society, Misanthrope Press, Pill Hill Press, and Murky Depths. He has managed to avoid winning a single award in this whole time and has decided to take that as an accolade in itself, whenever the tears stop falling.

He likes to think that his books are about real people who live in impossible worlds. Whether his books are Fantasy, Horror, Steampunk, or Sci-fi, Craig loves to go wherever the stories may take him.

Find the author via his website: craighallam.wordpress.com

Or tweet at him: @craighallam84

Or take a look at his Patreon page:

www.patreon.com/craighallam

More From This Author

Greaveburn

From the crumbling Belfry to the Citadel's stained-glass eye, across acres of cobbles streets and knotted alleyways that never see daylight, Greaveburn is a city with darkness at its core. Gothic spires battle for height, overlapping each other until the skyline is a jagged mass of thorns.

Under the cobbled streets lurk the Broken Folk, deformed rebels led by the hideously scarred Darrant, a man who once swore to protect the city. And in a darkened laboratory, the devious Professor Loosestrife builds a contraption known only as The Womb.

With Greaveburn being torn apart around her, can Abrasia avenge her father's murder before the Archduke's letter spells her doom?

Paperback ISBN: 978-1-908600-12-7
eBook ISBN: 978-1-908600-13-4

The Adventures of Alan Shaw

Escaping the workhouse was only the beginning of Alan Shaw's adventures.

For an orphan growing up on the streets of Victorian London, staying alive is a daily battle filled with choices a child should never have to make. Then Alan is offered more money than he can imagine; enough to take him to the new world and a new life. He only has to do one thing first – something that could bring the British Empire to a grinding halt.

In a series of adventures that take him from sea to sky, from Brighton to Bombay, Alan grows up in a steam-driven era where Automatons walk the streets of London and dirigibles master the air. Pitted against mad alchemists, tentacled submersibles, bomb-wielding saboteurs and the apocalyptic cult of the Ordo Fenris, Alan has his work cut out for him.

With a past as dark as his, who knows what Alan might grow up to be?

Paperback ISBN: 978-1-908600-32-5
eBook ISBN: 978-1-908600-33-2

Available from all major online and offline outlets.